# THE WORLD TURNED
# UPSIDE DOWN

# THE WORLD TURNED UPSIDE DOWN

## FINDING THE GOSPEL IN STRANGER THINGS

### MICHAEL S. HEISER

**LEXHAM PRESS**

*The World Turned Upside Down: Finding the Gospel in Stranger Things*

Copyright 2019 Michael S. Heiser

Lexham Press, 1313 Commercial St., Bellingham, WA 98225
LexhamPress.com

Print ISBN 9781683593225
Digital ISBN 9781683593232

Lexham Editorial: Derek R. Brown, Abigail Stocker, Danielle Thevenaz
Cover Design: Kristen Cork
Typesetting: ProjectLuz.com

TO THE MEMBERS OF MY TEENAGE PARTY:

SCOTT,
BRAD,
PAT,
TOM,
MARK,
AND RANDY

And Paul went in, as was his custom, and on three Sabbath days he reasoned with them from the Scriptures, explaining and proving that it was necessary for the Christ to suffer and to rise from the dead, and saying, "This Jesus, whom I proclaim to you, is the Christ." And some of them were persuaded and joined Paul and Silas, as did a great many of the devout Greeks and not a few of the leading women. But the Jews were jealous, and taking some wicked men of the rabble, they formed a mob, set the city in an uproar, and attacked the house of Jason, seeking to bring them out to the crowd. And when they could not find them, they dragged Jason and some of the brothers before the city authorities, shouting, **"These men who have turned the world upside down** have come here also, and Jason has received them, and they are all acting against the decrees of Caesar, saying that there is another king, Jesus."

**ACTS 17:2-7**

# CONTENTS

# CONTENTS

# PREFACE

The first season of *Stranger Things* premiered on July 15, 2016. There was no fanfare, no breathless anticipation generated by advance hype. Like other projects, the show was a Netflix™ experiment. Eight episodes later, it had exploded into an international sensation.

*Stranger Things* transports viewers back to 1983, more than a lifetime ago for many of the show's most devoted fans. Ronald Reagan was the president of the United States. The Washington Redskins won the Super Bowl (yes, that actually happened). *Return of the Jedi* was the highest-grossing movie of the year—which meant that *Star Wars* was already six years old. The Mario Bros. Nintendo arcade game debuted. Winona Ryder, the actress who plays Joyce Byers in *Stranger Things*, was twelve.

*Stranger Things* is set in the fictional town of Hawkins, Indiana. It's a quintessential small town: Everyone knows everyone else and wants to know their business. Nothing *really* bad ever happens; to quote the town's chief of police, Jim Hopper, the worst that had happened since he took over was "when an owl attacked Eleanor Gillespie's head because it thought that her hair was a nest." But this town also harbors secrets, and *Stranger Things* catapults its audience into one that would shake the entire town for years to come.

The first episode—and in many respects the entire show—revolves around the unexpected, eerie disappearance of Will Byers, Joyce's youngest son. As panic takes hold in the hearts of Will's family (his mother and his brother, Jonathan) and his three best friends (Mike Wheeler, Dustin Henderson, and Lucas Sinclair), an otherworldly evil—a grotesque creature Will's friends nickname "the Demogorgon"—infiltrates the town.

Not coincidentally, an equally sinister human threat emerges in tandem with the Demogorgon. Blame for the latter's appearance can be laid at the feet of a cabal of government operatives led by amoral scientist Dr. Martin Brenner, headquartered at Hawkins National Laboratory.

At first, things move along in all the familiar rhythms of life. As news of Will's disappearance circulates, people are sure the boy will be found. There are bullies to deal with at the middle school that Will and his friends attend. Nancy Wheeler—the sister of Will's friend, Mike—plots to deceive her parents for some unchaperoned time with her new boyfriend, Steve Harrington, the epic party boy at Hawkins High School. Nancy dismisses the concerns of her best friend, Barb Holland, who winds up in the wrong place at the wrong time because of Nancy and Steve. But the settled peace of the oblivious, sleepy town soon dissipates as the search for Will becomes a community project. The search is a tragic failure, save in one respect: it yields the discovery of peculiar girl with a shaved head who, when asked her name, points to the tattoo on her arm: 011. The boys quickly discover that there's more to her than a hesitancy to speak.

Eleven (or El for short) emerges as the central character of the series. As viewers suspect from the outset, she isn't your run-of-the-mill preteen girl. Her presence and her powers will forever alter the lives of those who know her. She is the key to understanding the real purpose of Hawkins National Laboratory, ostensibly run by the Energy Department for the mundane purpose of supplying the town with electricity. While the people of Hawkins might wonder why a power plant needs so much security, no one has any idea of what has transpired behind its gates and walls. But Eleven knows. Throughout the series she will save the rest of the characters tied to Will and his family from the beast and the "bad men" who are desperate to manage their mistake and maintain the secrecy of their experiments.

For me, *Stranger Things* is the perfect marriage of my interest in all things paranormal and the memory of my own teenage years along with the cast of characters among whom that life was lived. The combination calls to remembrance both questions I wondered about during those years and truths I was shown by the providence of God in answer. My hope is that this book will stimulate readers to discern what God really wants for them and how the good news of the gospel can be found as we reflect on the insightful, artful storytelling of *Stranger Things*.

# INTRODUCTION

**L**et me be honest. This book isn't propelled by any academic urge. I'm not a media critic. I just love *Stranger Things*. Before its creation I was fond of referring to *The X-Files* as the television event of my lifetime. I've been forced to change my thinking. I now say that *The X-Files* was the television event of my adulthood; *Stranger Things* has become the television event of my childhood.

That's anachronistic, of course. *Stranger Things* debuted well after *The X-Files*, and it's been a long time since I was a kid. But that's my point. *Stranger Things* takes me back to my childhood. The nostalgia that the show so skillfully cultivates seduces fans of the show who are my age. I see myself and my gang of friends in the characters. I relive the nerdy things we did (my middle- and high-school years were the seventies and eighties). My own kids talk about *Stranger Things* as though it was part of their own fondly remembered past. That's fine with me. They could be Googling worse things than what life was like in the '80s.

A lot about the fictional town of Hawkins, Indiana, and its middle school reminds me of growing up. When I watch the show I can see old neighborhoods and the store where we bought baseball cards, the kind that came with chewing gum that was essentially sliced granite. I relive the bike rides to school and my friends' houses. I can pick out middle-school friends and acquaintances—nerds, jocks, and the troubled bullies who spent most of their time in detention. Our school had an AV club. Most of the guys I hung out with had single parents. And I remember just about all of the movies that the series famously repurposes in weaving its earthy-but-ethereal tale of, well, the strange things going on in town. *Stranger Things* offers just the sort of terrifying-but-exhilarating adventure I would have wanted to get drawn into.

Turns out I was—and am—in that kind of adventure. All of us are. I'm talking about the paranormal conflict the Bible describes for the soul of every man, woman, and child that's raging beyond what our senses can detect. Demogorgons and Shadow Monsters on the other side of a supernatural Upside Down seek our misery and destruction. As viewers discern immediately, in *Stranger Things*, ignorance of or resistance to the mind-bending otherworldly manifestations doesn't make them untrue.

Many Christians resist or feel uneasy with the supernatural worldview of the Bible. I've written a good deal about the unseen realm and its place in the biblical worldview.[1] My goal has been to help people rediscover the Bible for what it is—a supernatural epic—and to stop reading it like it's a textbook. I've tried to convince people that the content of the Bible is either presented as story or framed by story, and that the Bible's story is inescapably supernatural.

That might sound odd. Why would Bible readers need to be convinced of such things? After all, many people who devote time to reading the Bible believe in God, Jesus, Satan, angels, and demons. While that's the case, the observation misses the point. There's a lot more going on in the Bible in the supernatural realm than these familiar figures. The Bible's supernatural intersection

---

1. I'm referring to the bestsellers *Supernatural: What the Bible Teaches about the Unseen World and Why It Matters* (Lexham Press, 2015); *The Unseen Realm: Recovering the Supernatural Worldview of the Bible* (Lexham Press, 2015); *Angels: What the Bible Really Says about God's Heavenly Host* (Lexham Press, 2018); *Demons: What the Bible Really Says about the Powers of Darkness* (Lexham Press, forthcoming); and *Reversing Hermon: Enoch, the Watchers, and the Forgotten Mission of Jesus Christ* (2nd ed: Lexham Press, 2019).

of an animate, spiritual world with the terrestrial human reality transcends what you would typically hear in church.

## THE GOSPEL ISN'T AS DULL AS WE MAKE IT

When Bible scholars talk about the gospel, it's usually in a dialect of academese. We like to spell out what the gospel is and isn't propositionally. We point out that the Greek term translated "gospel" (*euangelion*) means "good news." The "good news" refers to how Jesus' death, burial, and resurrection are the basis for the forgiveness of our sins and everlasting life for all who trust in that message. And the gospel really is good news because we all sin (Rom 3:23) and, without the gospel, will not have everlasting life in God's presence (Rom 6:23; John 3:16). *We have to be made acceptable to God.* That's what the cross accomplished, if we will only believe it (Rom 5:6–8; Eph 2:8–9).

But that's just a definition. You could put it on an index card and memorize it for a Bible doctrine course. It's like reading a synopsis of *Harry Potter* or *Lord of the Rings* instead of reading the full stories (or watching the movies, for that matter).

It's not only scholars who are guilty of presenting the gospel in prose that would be at home on an FAQ web page. Ask most people in church to tell you what the Bible is about, and odds are good that you'll get something like this: "The Bible is about God's plan of salvation for humankind. God created humanity. Humans fell into sin and inherited death in the process. God forgave them and eventually got around to choosing Israel to be his own people. Israel went astray (like everyone else) but produced the Messiah, Jesus. Jesus died on the cross to secure forgiveness, and his followers preached that message through-out the world. That's what we're supposed to do, too, until Jesus returns to judge the world and take believers to heaven forever." There you go—something else to put on an index card (or two).

That paragraph hits important ideas but doesn't give you any sense of the supernatural conflict that is running in the background on nearly every page of the Bible (and which takes center stage in a lot of its scenes). But that's the way most people—most *Christians*—have the story of the Bible presented to them.

It's a shame that this is the case. On the one hand, it's good that we encounter the fact that the cross is the sole means of salvation for us all. On the other hand, it's kind of dull. It's *bookish*. To be blunt, that paragraph would be entirely appropriate for a textbook about the Bible. Class is in session! Stay awake, because there may be a quiz when we're done.

While our dull-as-dishwater paragraph is on target, it skips the most enthralling supernatural aspects of the biblical story. It presents nothing that captures the imagination. *That* is what well-told stories do, and the Bible is certainly a story told well.

## THE GOSPEL STORY IN ITS SUPERNATURAL CONTEXT

The Bible tells the story of how God wanted a human family. When God decided to create a human family for himself, he wasn't alone. God already had a supernatural family—and I'm *not* talking about the Trinity. God already had *children*. These "sons of God" were spectators when he laid the foundations of the world (Job 38:4–7).

God's supernatural children were also his audience at the moment described in Genesis 1:26 ("Let *us* make humankind in *our* image and according to *our* likeness," LEB). God wasn't talking to the members of the Trinity. They didn't need the information. They are co-eternal and co-omniscient (at least in any form of orthodox Christian teaching). Rather than the Trinity, God was talking to his supernatural children. That's one reason why there are plurals in the verse.

God was, in effect, telling his celestial children, "Let's have more children in our family! Let's make them like us!" When God actually added humans to his family, he was the only one who did the creating ("So God created humankind in *his* image, in the likeness of God *he created* him, male and female *he created* them"; Gen 1:27 LEB). The plurals in Genesis 1:26 loop humanity's supernatural siblings into the drama of God's new creation.

God's wish in this scene is understandable. The Bible's story begins with creation, but among all the life forms God had planned for life on earth, none was capable of having a relationship with him. Plants, animals, bacteria, etc. couldn't converse with God, share thoughts with God, or express love and appreciation to God.

God decided to change that circumstance. He made creatures with whom he could commune and interact, intellectually and spiritually, and who could also partner with him in maintaining and enjoying this wonderful new world. To do that God shared his abilities—like self-awareness, reason, intuition, and free will—with these new creatures, humanity.

God's decision frames the rest of the Bible's story. As embodied children, God would have to come to humanity so that they could enjoy him. They couldn't come to him. And so God took up residence on earth in a garden called Eden, where he had put his earthly children.

The story took a sad, painful turn very quickly. Adam and Eve, earth's first human couple, sinned against God. They were deceived by a supernatural apostate, a member of God's heavenly family who had decided that what God wanted wasn't what he wanted. God's vision for a human family was shattered. His earthly children were now estranged from him, destined under the curse of death to be separated from him forever. Humanity would grow up in a broken home in a deadly, chaotic world.

But the fall isn't the only reason why the world is the mess that it is. The subplot of evil in the biblical story proceeds on multiple fronts. The fall was the first of *three* reasons for the human dilemma. Most Christians are only taught about this first one. As Eden recedes into the background, the threat to humanity has not been eliminated. Eventually demons are spawned, and the earth is enslaved in the wake of two other rebellions by the heavenly sons of God (Gen 6:1–4; Deut 32:8). The alert reader senses there's an unseen black, demonic Hydra watching through a thin preternatural veil, waiting for its malevolent opportunity. If you've seen *Stranger Things,* that should sound familiar.

## NOW FOR THE GOOD NEWS

God's persistent, unyielding yearning to have a human family compelled him not to give up on calling his children back. His visitation of Abraham, a lone stream of light penetrating the thickening darkness, would lead to the birth of the One the apostle Paul called the ultimate seed of Abraham, born to redeem the sons and daughters of earth in the fullness of time (Gal 3:15–16, 26–29; 4:4–6).

It's no accident, then, that the coming of Jesus was referred to as "good news" in the New Testament. It's also no accident that, in addition to presenting what happened on the cross as the exclusive means of God's forgiveness and everlasting life in God's family (John 3:16; 14:6), it is also cast as the decisive defeat of the powers of darkness. In other words, there's a reason why, when Paul talks about the resurrection, he links it to the end of authority of the supernatural rulers and powers in control of the nations (Rom 8:37–39; Eph 1:20–23; 1 Pet 3:22).

As I've chronicled in other books, there are dozens of passages in the Bible that frame everything from geography to baptism in terms of supernatural warfare. The story of the gospel is framed by a supernatural worldview. The same is true of *Stranger Things*.

Though the series is not driven by theology, its plotline is propelled by the looming threat of a malevolent, otherworldly intelligence that seeks the destruction of all that the characters hold dear. I'm not going to make an argument that the hit series is "about" the biblical story line or follows it in any deliberate way. It doesn't. Rather, I want readers to discern that there is a lot of material in *Stranger Things* that is analogous to the Bible's long story of God's desire for a human family and of the supernatural agents bent on its failure or fulfillment.

## THE GOOD NEWS AND
## *STRANGER THINGS*

As the Bible's story unfolds, it becomes clear that it is propelled by God's love, shown in his unstoppable pursuit of a human family. *Family* is also at the heart of *Stranger Things*. From Eleven's forlorn, isolated existence, to the relentless search for Will, to Hopper's tragic loss, every character in the show yearns for the companionship and love that secure family relationships bring. The Demogorgon and the unearthly overlord of the Upside Down aim to destroy the characters and their solidarity through literal violence or imperceptible deception and manipulation. Yet these same threats draw the heroes together, because they cannot defeat evil by themselves. At the center of the clash is an opposing power, resident in the most unlikely source, brought to the fore by abuse, whose blood is a sign of healing, protection, and deliverance.

This paragraph should alert anyone who is vaguely familiar with the story of salvation through Jesus to the similarities between the gospel and *Stranger Things*. At the end of season 1 Eleven conquered the horrific Demogorgon and saved her friends but at a very high cost. She had disappeared into the Upside Down, the realm of death. Hawkins was safe, but all was not well. Will Byers had been infected by the pathogenic Upside Down. Something even more sinister loomed on the horizon.

Understandably, season 2 opened with the kids in the Party resigned to the loss of Eleven—except for Mike. His love for her kept his faith alive. Viewers knew that Eleven had already escaped the Upside Down, but she had returned to a world where her friends were in lethal danger. A cancerous malignancy was spreading through Hawkins, rotting the very ground under the town. The Shadow Monster would possess and manipulate Will to lead a newly spawned hive-mind horde of "Demodogs" to destroy everyone Eleven had saved. She had escaped death, but her ability to rescue her friends was now impeded by Hopper's resistance, born of his fear at the prospect of another terrible loss. He lacked faith in her character and power. She would leave and return in a different, yet the same, form to overpower darkness once more.

Those familiar with the story of Jesus know that the story doesn't end with the cross. Initially the loss of Jesus plunged his friends and followers into deep depression. They believed their dream of the Messiah, finally come, was over. But Jesus rose from the tomb, escaping the grip of death. The cross and resurrection brought forgiveness of sin and the promise of everlasting life for those who believe.

When he rose from the dead, Jesus returned to a world still permeated with the contagion of sin. Satan's claim on the souls of humanity and the ruling authority of the powers of darkness had been nullified. But these events were only the inauguration of a long struggle against cosmic opposition. The powers of darkness refused to surrender. The followers of Jesus, tasked with taking the message of the gospel to the world, would soon be under siege. He would leave but return as the Spirit, yet still be distinct from the Spirit (Acts 16:6–7; Phil 1:19; 1 Pet 1:11; Gal 4:6; 2 Cor 3:17–18). The Spirit would be an ever-present Helper (John 14:16) to combat depravity (Rom 8:4; Gal 5:16), resist the dark cosmic powers (Eph 6:12), and protect them from the one who sought to devour them (1 Pet 5:8). Where two or three were gathered, he would be there in their midst (Matt 18:20). His presence was sufficient—if they would believe.

Even the end of season 2 resonates with the New Testament story. The hellish gate had been closed, but all is *still* not well in Hawkins. The final scene of the second season of *Stranger Things* leaves viewers with the assurance that Eleven would be there for those who need her, present in their midst, but that didn't mean safety and security. The Shadow Monster had been defeated, not destroyed, and his designs were undeterred.

## STRANGE EXPECTATIONS

*Stranger Things* doesn't intentionally retell the gospel story. The Duffer brothers, the show's creators, had nothing of that sort in mind. But the fact that the story has so many points of analogy to the saga of Jesus and his followers against the powers of darkness isn't coincidental. Truth often works off the radar. The story of God's love for us contains all the compelling archetypal elements and questions that have fueled human contemplation and tapped into its deepest yearnings for millennia. Is there a

God who made us and loves us? Did this God have a purposeful destiny in mind for us? Is there life after death? Conversely, are there otherworldly threats to our welfare? Why is there evil? Can evil be overcome?

Mythic genres like fantasy and science fiction allow story-tellers to play off the supernatural and utopian impulses of their readers, consciously or unconsciously. *Stranger Things* does this exceedingly well. As for the gospel, we should not be surprised that, recollecting a conversation with J. R. R. Tolkien and Hugo Dyson, C. S. Lewis was led to faith by the realization that "the story of Christ is simply a true myth: a myth working on us in the same way as the others, but with this tremendous difference that it *really happened.*"[2]

*Stranger Things* taps into spiritual questions and crises and addresses them the way the gospel story does—with mystery and transcendent power, justice, and love. The goal of this book is to discern elements of *Stranger Things* that make us think about the story of Jesus and which draw attention to God's salvation plan. For those familiar with the New Testament story of Jesus, we'll see in the pages that follow that the show offers compelling, imaginative portrayals of important spiritual truths. For others, *Stranger Things* can plant the seeds of the gospel of Jesus Christ—the myth that is true.

In the interest of accomplishing this goal, the chapters of the book are topical, not chronological. That is, the chapters do not simply move through the episodes of each season of *Stranger Things* in the order in which they occurred; each chapter is oriented by one spiritual truth. In the course of examining how *Stranger Things* conveys that truth in its own memorable ways, I will appeal to a variety of episodes. For reasons that will be

---

2. C. S. Lewis, letter to Arthur Greeves, October 18, 1931.

evident in reading, chapter 7 marks the transition from season 1 to season 2. Consequently, chapters 1–6 and 7–11 still preserve the basic flow of the show's storytelling, observing how the series connects points of its own larger plot and further develops the characters.

# 1

## AS LOST AS
## WILL BYERS

## THE NEED TO BELONG

The very first episode of *Stranger Things* is entitled, "The Vanishing of Will Byers." It's a perfect beginning. The cryptic circumstances of Will's abduction reveal just enough to let us know that something otherworldly is its cause. We'll learn that Will is "here but not here," trapped in a parallel universe, an unnatural world that is ultimately lethal to all who cross over into it. Three realizations flash through our minds and hearts in the wake of the tragic event: the pain of loss, the threat of death, and the impossibility of changing the situation. We'll consider all of those disturbing intuitions in the ensuing chapters, but it is the first that will capture our attention here, at the outset.

Just as important as Will's vanishing, we're immediately introduced to the tight-knit group of boys that will propel the series: Will Byers, Dustin Henderson, Mike Wheeler, and Lucas Sinclair. The fact that the "Party" (as they refer to themselves) is playing Dungeons and Dragons (D&D) in the opening scene not only portends the Demogorgon—a dreaded, lethal enemy that, unknown to them, has entered their reality—but anticipates what we'll learn of their commitment to each other.

In the middle-school terminology of the eighties, the four are "nerds"—outcasts among their peers. They are united by the shared status of being uncool due to their mutual love for D&D, AV gadgetry, comic books, video games, and science fiction. I could immediately identify with them.

## FAMILIAR THINGS

My own small cadre of friends formed our own club, complete with meetings, infrastructure planning, and (of course) hats. While I was into comic books and science fiction, my real obsession at their age was a statistics-based baseball board game called APBA—it was fantasy baseball before there was such a thing. True to form, I and my friends conducted ten-hour (or more) APBA marathons just like the Party's D&D session that opens the first season of the show. Truth be told, we spent almost *two years* replaying the 1973 baseball season. Why? Because we wanted to see how realistic the replay was. It was an experiment. Geeky kids do those sorts of things.

Fortunately, my Party never lost a member, at least until we reached college age. But we had all suffered losses. My father left my mother when I was five and my brother three. For years I wondered if I had somehow contributed to the breakup, whether I had been a burden in some way. It was a misguided thought, but children don't exactly have the capacity to reason deeply about such complicated things as divorce. When my mom remarried, it was to an alcoholic. My best friend had a similar story, though that divorce had a more clear-cut rationale: his dad couldn't stand being married to a "Jesus freak." The divorce of my friend's parents left him and his three siblings, two of whom had cystic fibrosis, with insufficient support. To say they struggled would be a dramatic understatement. But it was in their home that I first heard the gospel, and it was through the influence of that friend that I came to believe its message as a teenager.

With one exception, each of my other middle-school friends also came from broken homes, one of which was also plagued by alcoholism. We each coped differently with what would now be clinically termed "detachment disorder," defined by one source as "an inability to connect with others on an emotional level, as well as a means of coping with anxiety by avoiding certain situations that trigger it."[1] Our homes were a mess, but we had each other. We were a unit—a Party.

## EVERYONE IS BROKEN A LITTLE

This sort of brokenness is at the heart of *Stranger Things*. Each member of the Party—really, every major character in the show—has a battle to wage against loneliness, lack of acceptance, fear of being unwanted, or tragic personal loss that makes them who they are.

When Will Byers goes missing, we are introduced to his family. His mom, Joyce, is a harried single mom who becomes absolutely frantic to find her son. Will's brother, Jonathan, is a loner who carries resentment toward his father, Lonnie, for abandoning them. Joyce and Jonathan carry the guilt of not being at home on the night that Will vanishes due to the burden of cobbling jobs together to make ends meet. Joyce's irrational refusal to accept another loss, even when the authorities recover a body, conveys a woman teetering between psychosis and unquenchable faith.

We are eventually introduced to Dustin's broken home (he lives with his mom; his father is never mentioned) and the pathological detachment of Mike's father in basically every regard. The only family not torn apart by divorce and tragedy is Lucas's, but as he is African-American in a lily-white small town, his own consciousness of otherness leaks through in both sad and comical ways. The jaded, alcoholic, womanizing chief of police, Jim Hopper, lost his only daughter, Sara, to cancer in her early years; the tragedy haunts him throughout the show but steels him in his pursuit of Will and justice against the evil

---

1. Quotation from ScienceDaily.com.

engulfing Hawkins. Emotional destitution and yearning for deep relationship are threads that run through Nancy Wheeler's guilt over the death of her friend Barb, her vacillating feelings for Steve, and her developing bond with Jonathan.

## SOME PEOPLE ARE BROKEN A LOT

As wistful and poignant as these backstories are, they pale next to that of the central character of *Stranger Things*. Eleven is the show's archetypal figure of adversity, neglect, and exploitation. Our first glimpse of her occurs a little over halfway through the first episode. No sooner does the creepy Dr. Brenner pronounce "she can't have gone far" after assessing the destructive aftermath of a mysterious lab catastrophe than the scene cuts to a barefoot girl in the woods, clothed only in a tattered lab gown, face smudged with dirt, her head shorn. Hungry, she sneaks into the back of Benny's Burgers, a Hawkins greasy-spoon where fried food and local gossip dominate the menu, to forage for food. In a few minutes she's caught in the act by Benny, who tries to help her and later pays the price for doing so at the hand of the seemingly pleasant woman from social services who's actually a government assassin.

The Eleven we meet can barely communicate. We quickly see that, even in the company of friends, her vocabulary is limited and her social skills nonexistent. She has lived all her life in a cloistered, clinical environment, cut off from ordinary human interaction and relationships. When Mike asks her what her name is, she can only identify herself by the numerical tattoo on her arm. Not only do we learn that she's been deprived of the most basic human psychological needs—companionship, trust, loyalty, and love—but she was punished for disobedience to her overlord, "Papa," with further isolation.

While searching for Will in the pouring rain, Lucas, Mike, and Dustin stumble upon Eleven in the woods behind Hawkins National Laboratory ("Mirkwood"), which is adjacent to the Byers house. The boys are naturally stunned to find the girl, drenched and shivering, clad only in an oversize T-shirt. In ensuing episodes we witness Eleven encounter television, recliners, and Mike's toys for the first time; her reactions range from wonder to bored disinterest. Eleven gives every indication that she's utterly disoriented by anything we and the rest of the characters would consider normal.

Given my own backstory the show's plotlines struck chords of memory. Though I got along with everyone I knew, I was a broken kid. Things weren't the way they were supposed to be. But what I hadn't known until I heard the gospel was that I was as lost as Will Byers. It isn't long before we learn that Will is trapped in another reality plane, the Upside Down. He's powerless to escape. His condition is irreversible. Without the intervention of a greater power and someone courageous enough to seek what was lost, he will die and be forever separated from those he loved and who loved him. Without Christ, that is our destiny—it was my destiny.

## CREATED TO BELONG

The Bible teaches that alienation from the God who made us and loved us is a tragic anomaly in God's intended world. Will Byers found himself in an anti-world, a bizarre, abnormal place foreign to human inclusion and experience. We're no different. Estrangement from our Father and his home is an unnatural condition that's out of step with what God wanted from the very beginning.

Think about how the Bible's story begins. When God created humankind, he was acting intentionally. We know that God wasn't trying to fill some deficiency in himself. His perfection rules that out (Ps 18:30; Matt 5:48). God wanted us to exist in order to enjoy us and to have us enjoy him in return.

Because the Bible teaches that human life is God's creation, it's no surprise that God is portrayed as "Father" and all human beings as his "children" (Acts 17:26–29). Adam was God's "son" (Luke 3:38). The people of Israel (Exod 4:22) and Israel's king (Psalm 2:7) are described as God's sons. Those who embrace the gospel are the children of God (John 1:12).

Think about that vocabulary. What's the context for words like "Father" and "children"? *Family*. While this observation might seem elementary, the beginning of this thread tends to be hidden in plain sight for many Bible readers. The Bible tells us that before God created humanity he already had children. The Bible calls them "sons of God." We call them angels. They were God's supernatural family. They were here before humans. They "shouted for joy" as they watched God lay the foundations of the earth (Job 38:4–7).

The fact that God already had a supernatural family provides some clarity for his motivation for creating us. God wanted a human family in addition to his heavenly family. The biblical story of Eden has God coming to earth with his celestial children. God speaks to them a few times in the story (Gen 1:26; 3:22).[2] Tragically, one of them appeared to Eve in the form of a serpent to undermine God's wishes (Gen 3:1–7; 2 Cor 11:3; Rev 12:9; 20:2). His deception brings death into the human world God created.

Eden was where heaven came to earth. It was God's home on earth. When God created Adam and placed him in Eden (Gen 2:15), God wanted his two families to live together with him. This

---

2. I discuss the evidence for this and its implications at length in *The Unseen Realm: Recovering the Supernatural Worldview of the Bible* (Lexham Press, 2015), 44–82.

means that, just like God's heavenly children, humans were originally created as fit for the presence of God himself. God wanted his children with him. Creation was about family.

## MADE LIKE GOD TO BE WITH GOD

When we reflect on the Eden story this way, the details of the wider Genesis story come into focus. God had done a lot of creating by the time he got to Adam and Eve: plants, insects, flying creatures, and land animals. As marvelous as they were, none of those creatures was capable of having a relationship with its Maker. They could not share their thoughts with God. They could not express love and gratitude. That's what members of a family do (or are supposed to do). They form relationships that transcend biology. They connect intellectually and emotionally. They form companionship bonds. As spectacular as plants and animals are, they could not reciprocate in these ways. *They weren't family*.

There was a clear solution to this problem: God needed to create something like himself in order to have what he really wanted. "So God created man in his own image, in the image of God he created him; male and female he created them" (Gen 1:27). The image of God is an important concept in the Bible. Human beings—unlike any other created thing on earth—were created to be like God. This actually refers to a status and not a specific ability.[3] Think of the "image" of God as a verb, and you'll get the idea. We were created to image God, to be his imagers—to represent him or be his proxy to each other and to all the earth.

Think about the implications of all that. Being created as imagers of God gives each of us a secure, profound identity. It was God's original desire that every human being would be his child and partner. *That* is how God looks at us. Imaging God also

---

3. See Heiser, *Unseen Realm*, 38–43, for discussion and documentation.

gives us purpose. We have a mission. Every person, no matter how small or weak or short-lived, has some role to play in someone else's life. Often that happens in invisible, unspectacular ways. That's actually the way that God works most of the time, with an unseen hand.

The Bible's story opens with family. God desired to be the Father of both his families and have them all be with him in his new, wonderful, terrestrial home. But the desire of God's heart didn't last long. It was soon hopelessly broken by deception and rebellion. Death became the new, overriding reality.

## HEALING WHAT'S BROKEN

This crushing loss and hopeless future is the entry point for the gospel. It may sound odd, but many Christians have lost a sense of what it means to be without Christ. Many churches present the gospel in such a way that the answer to why we even need it is forgotten. We need the gospel because we are estranged from God. As Adam and Eve were driven from Eden (Gen 3:22–24), we have been expelled from God's home. We are spiritual orphans—we're under the curse of the fall and our own sin (Rom 5:12). In Paul's words, we "[have] no hope and [are] without God in the world" (Eph 2:12). We are "alienated from the life of God" (Eph 4:18). It's an ugly picture, but the New Testament doesn't leave us there. We were not only originally created to be with God, but God never abandoned that goal.

The "gospel"—the good news—is that God saw our self-induced condition and loved us just the same. God sent his Son, Jesus, for our salvation. Believing the good news about who Jesus is and what he did on the cross is the only means we have to be restored to God's family (John 3:16; 14:6). According to the apostle Paul, when we believe God's plan to bring us back home, he adopts us as his children (Gal 4:5; Eph 1:5). Because God does this, we have a "home" with the Lord (2 Cor 5:8), a "house not made with hands, eternal in the heavens" (2 Cor 5:1). The apostle John revels in the insight, "See what kind of love the Father has given to us, that we should be called children of God; and so we are" (1 John 3:1).

## THE RIGHT-SIDE UP

*Stranger Things* communicates the pain of loss and estrangement in visceral, moving ways. The loss of Will draws us into the pain of those who love him. Their loss triggers the deep yearning inside of us all to have things set right. All of us want to know who we are, why we're here, and where we truly belong. But the search for Will has just begun. It's heartbreaking to watch the characters drawn toward the terrible but obvious realization that their efforts are pointless. We must awaken to the fact that the heart of God aches for all those who still need to embrace the gospel in the same way. Without the gospel, God knows they're as lost as Will Byers, cut off from him in our own Upside Down.

# THE VALE OF
# SHADOWS

# TRAPPED IN A HOSTILE WORLD

L ocating and rescuing Will propels the first season of *Stranger Things*. The desperation of his friends and family escalates with every scene. But it's time to consider Will's vanishing from *his* perspective. Unless someone finds him, he's going to die, and he knows it. Will is trapped in the realm of death. The Demogorgon pursues him relentlessly. He is quite literally being stalked by death. Will knows it's only a matter of time before he can't hide anymore. He grows weaker with every effort to evade the monster. By the time Eleven locates him in Castle Byers in the Upside Down to tell him his mom is coming, he can barely mumble, "Hurry."

## UNDER A CURSE

Like Will, without the gospel we are estranged from the secure home we desperately need and want. But that's only part of our predicament. We're living under the sentence of death, both physically and spiritually, a twofold by-product of our estrangement from God.

The Bible speaks to both kinds of death. Death entered God's world because of Adam's fall, a failure that resulted in death being "spread to all men" (Rom 5:12). We will return to dust (Gen 2:19; 3:19; Ps 104:29). As if the prospect of earthly mortality weren't troubling enough, the Bible tells us that, if we do not embrace the gospel, we will subsequently suffer what the Bible calls the "second death," eternal separation from the presence of God (Rev 20:6, 14).

This really doesn't do justice to the tragic nature of our situation, though. We are not only under a curse and estranged from the God who loves us, but we deserve the results that follow. Every human being since Adam is "dead in ... trespasses and sins" (Eph 2:1, 5). Because we lack God's perfect nature we all sin—that is, we fail to align to God's moral character in what we do, say, and think. As the prophet Isaiah described, we are like sheep gone astray, every one of us turning to his or her own way (Isa 53:6). The result is not only falling short of what God designed us to be (Rom 3:23) but death in this life and everlasting separation from a holy God in the next life (Rom 6:23).

But the human vices cataloged in the Bible show that sin is not only about wandering away from what God wants in our own character—it's humanity's bent toward self-destruction and looking out for ourselves at the expense of others. Among the things we do to make ourselves and others miserable and embittered are sexual immorality, debauchery, hatred, discord, jealousy, rage, selfish ambition, factiousness, and envy. We each might think we're the exception, but the Bible warns us (for our own good) that our hearts are "deceitful above all things, and desperately sick" (Jer 17:9). We can't expect anything else from life without God. We're hopelessly imperfect people trapped in a world that isn't what it was supposed to be.

## DEATH PERSONIFIED

The predicament of Will Byers is a useful metaphor for our spiritual conundrum: he's trapped, too. At first, "Upside Down" is a neutral term that doesn't necessarily evoke fear. The kids in the Party adopt it because of the pen-and-paper object lesson about the flea and the acrobat offered by their science teacher, Mr. Clarke, who also runs the AV Club. Their teacher's explanation reminds them of Eleven's earlier attempt to explain Will's whereabouts by flipping the D&D board upside down.

But the kids in the Party won't experience the Upside Down until season 2. For them it's only theory. They don't comprehend it as a terrible place until their Bard speaks to the issue after doing some research. It is Dustin's analogy, the "Vale of Shadows," that vividly captures what we see in every scene in the Upside Down. In one scene, he reads from his copy of the *D&D Expert Rulebook*:

> The Vale of Shadows is a dimension that is a dark reflection, or echo, of our world. It is a place of decay and death, a plane out of phase, a place with monsters. It is right next to you and you don't even see it.

The Upside Down, or Vale of Shadows, is indeed a dark "place of decay and death." In the Vale it is always night, never day. Its very air is permeated with particles of its own putrefaction, slowly asphyxiating those unfortunate or foolish enough to enter. Roots on and within the ground of the Vale are alive, waiting to seize their smothered prey. The Vale is darkness, devouring, and death.

The Demogorgon belongs to the Vale of Shadows. The malformed monster is drawn out by blood. In biblical thought, blood is the life force (Lev 17:11, 14). Lose enough of it, and death comes. The Demogorgon is not the *Stranger Things* version of the devil or Satan. The Shadow Monster ("Mind Flayer") is a more apt counterpart to the devil, given its intelligence, its possession of Will, and its command of the other denizens of the Vale. The Demogorgon is instead the personification of the Vale of

Shadows. It is darkness personified and walking, an agile consumer of life bent on reversing God's gift of life in our creation.[1]

Season 2 replaces the Demogorgon with dozens of smaller versions—"Demodogs," as Dustin annoyingly reminds anyone who is listening. Unlike the Demogorgon, these preternatural mutations travel on all fours and hunt in packs. But their hunger for blood is just as insatiable. They feed on their prey at a place Mike and Steve refer to as "the Hub," the spot where underground tunnels extending from the Gate beneath Hawkins lab fuse.

That the tunnel network is an extension of the Vale of Shadows is everywhere evident. The same putridity pervades the air. The floors, walls, and ceilings of every inch yearn to squeeze the life out of the living. Even outside the Upside Down every form of plant life with roots touching the network's toxic contagion rots.

## LIVING DARKNESS

Christians typically think of the realm of everlasting death as hellfire. While certain passages in the Bible include that element (Matt 5:22; Mark 9:43), other descriptions of the afterlife realm of the dead sound a lot like the Vale of Shadows—complete with its monsters.

Perhaps the most familiar language in that regard comes from Psalm 23:4 ("even though I walk through the valley of the shadow of death"). The phrase "shadow of death" is an Old Testament Hebrew term understood as meaning "very deep

---

1. It is tempting to think that the creators of *Stranger Things* drew the term "Demogorgon" from the writings of Milton, where it appears as one of several personifications expressing Satan's goal: the de-creation of God's beautiful order to chaos and darkness (*Paradise Lost* ii. 961–965). See A. B. Chambers, "Chaos in Paradise Lost," *Journal of the History of Ideas* 24:1 (1963): 55–84 (esp. 66).

shadow" or "total darkness."[2] The imagery is similar to some of Jesus' later descriptions of where lost souls end up: "outer darkness" (Matt 8:12; 22:13; 25:30). The realm of death in biblical thought is the epitome of darkness (Job 17:13; 18:18). It is unfathomably distant from the light of God's presence. The realm of the dead was entered through the grave, from which no one escapes. Hence, the grave is described as "the pit ... the regions dark and deep" (Ps 88:6) that has "cords," "snares," and "bars" to imprison its inhabitants (2 Sam 22:6; Ps 18:5; Job 17:16).

The most common term for the realm of the dead is a Hebrew word found in the Old Testament. In some English translations the word is not translated but merely transliterated—the representation of characters or words from one language in characters or words of another language—into English letters: *Sheol* (see Ps 88:3–5). As the realm of the disembodied dead, it has no literal latitude and longitude. It is a placeless place. Sheol is at times personified in the Old Testament as a barren womb (that is, a place where there is no life; Prov 30:16) or an insatiable beast, eager to devour anyone it encounters (Isa 5:14; Prov 1:12; 27:20; Ps 141:7). The infamous Rephaim, the disembodied giant warrior-kings of old, called Sheol their home. They were thought of as demons, "bastard spirits" in the days of Jesus.[3]

The Vale of Shadows is a vivid metaphor communicating hostility to life. People of the biblical world thought of the desert wilderness in the same way. The desert was, to human experience, barren and dangerous, void of food and water, and filled with threats and nocturnal creatures considered "unclean" because they fed on corpses.

---

2. Peter C. Craigie, *Psalms 1–50*, 2nd ed., Word Biblical Commentary 19 (Nashville: Thomas Nelson, 2004), 207.

3. See Heiser, *Demons* (Bellingham, WA: Lexham Press, forthcoming), chapter 1.

The wilderness served as a metaphor for the realm of the dead and its citizens. In the Old Testament, the wilderness was the home of Azazel, considered prince of demons and a Satan figure in Jesus' day. On the Day of Atonement, the goat "for Azazel" was driven into the wilderness, carrying the sins of the nation back to where they belonged (Lev 16:7–10). Azazel was accompanied by "goat demons" (Lev 17:7). The metaphor even extended to cities rendered uninhabitable by conquest. The prophesied end of Babylon, the empire that conquered Jerusalem and sent the Israelites into captivity, is cast as a desert wilderness in the wake of God's judgment. Its vitality would be extinguished. It would become home to otherworldly phantoms who come at night in the guise of "wild animals," "howling creatures," and "owls" (Isa 13:21–22; 34:11–15; Jer 50:39).

It should not surprise us that in the New Testament Jesus is driven into the desert wilderness to be tempted by Satan (Matt 4:1; Mark 1:12–13). Because of the Old Testament association of the desert wilderness with demons and death, Satan's appearance there would not strike readers as unexpected. Likewise, the demon possessed did not live in cities, where life normally took place. They dwelt in tombs out in the arid hill country (Matt 8:28; Mark 5:5). When men apprehended them, they broke free and were "driven ... into the desert" (Luke 8:29). Exorcised demons also sought the wilderness, the "waterless places" (Luke 11:24; Matt 12:43). These descriptions are all the more telling—and connected to the Old Testament realm of the dead—when one realizes that the Judaism of Jesus' day taught that demons were the disembodied spirits of dead Rephaim giants.[4]

---

4. Heiser, *Demons*, chapters 5, 6, and 10.

## THE RIGHT-SIDE UP

In the Bible, the realm of the dead was a fearful place that everyone would visit, because *everyone dies*. Like Sheol, the Vale of Shadows and its personification, the Demogorgon, are insatiable. Nevertheless, it was the hope of the righteous to be lifted out of Sheol (1 Sam 2:6; Pss 30:3; 49:15). But we must be honest with the severity of our predicament. Doing so prepares us for the next, difficult but essential spiritual lesson: that the solution to our dilemma can only be found outside ourselves. Resistance to that reality displaces and impedes faith, for salvation through the gospel of Jesus Christ is not about faith in ourselves but faith in the supernatural accomplishments of someone exponentially greater.

*Stranger Things* prepares our hearts for this lesson. Will Byers hoped to escape the Upside Down. He knew he could not save himself, and so he reached out to his mother in an assortment of spectral ways, hoping she would understand and save him. But viewers learn that Joyce could not save him either without paranormal intervention. As we'll see, Will himself came to understand this as well. In the end his deliverance was contingent upon, and enabled by, otherworldly power.

# FROM ONE BLACK HOLE TO ANOTHER

# WE CAN'T SAVE OURSELVES

Coping with personal pain and failure takes different forms: We can throw ourselves into worthy pursuits or sinful self-destruction. We might overcompensate and perpetuate the self-delusion that we can change the unchangeable, or we might yield to rage. One path leads to self-deception, the other to self-loathing. We don't realize it, but we make things worse.

## CYCLES OF FAILURE

No character in *Stranger Things* typifies this struggle more transparently than Hawkins's chief of police, Jim Hopper. He's a tortured soul. The Hopper of season 1 is caught in a cycle of self-loathing. The loss of his little daughter Sara to cancer and the subsequent unraveling of his marriage have driven him to cynicism. He hints to Joyce in one scene, "That PTSD stuff, that's real," and tries unconvincingly to tell her that the pain of losing a child will "get better." What helps Hopper "get better"? Alcohol, anti-depression drugs, and sleeping around with the women of Hawkins.

Our understanding of his suffering grows as the series moves along. The Hopper of season 2 is trapped in self-delusion. Like so many people desperate to reverse some irreversible circumstance in life, Hopper becomes obsessively overprotective of Eleven, whom he has rescued from the woods outside Hawkins after her escape from the Upside Down. Eleven becomes a surrogate for Sara, Hopper's lost daughter. This is telegraphed poignantly in season 2, where Hopper wears Sara's blue hair tie around his wrist—something he does only in the wake of meeting Eleven at the end of season 1. Hopper ends up giving the wristband to Eleven (she wears it at the Snow Ball). The message is clear: he cannot lose her and repeat the past; he is reimagining his past through her. He must regain what he lost. He has to fix his life.

Hopper convinces himself that he must not allow Eleven's whereabouts to be known—even to Mike and the rest of the Party, her closest friends. His strategy is to quarantine her in his cabin. While his intentions are good, Hopper fails as a father, suffocating Eleven with isolation, breaking promises and misleading her. Every viewer knows that, for Eleven, these circumstances are reverberations of her own suffering. Predictably, Eleven will not tolerate being sequestered and lied to, and she abandons the cabin and Hopper. She later returns, driven by her realization that the ones she loves will die unless she does.

Toward the end of season 2, Hopper and Eleven reconcile. Once he realizes he was wrong and had undermined their relationship, he confesses, "A lot of things I shouldn't have done. Sometimes I feel like I'm ... like I'm just some kind of black hole or something ... [that] sucks everything towards it and destroys it." He's right in a way. When we can't quite come to the end of ourselves and admit we need help instead of trying to change the unchangeable, we make things worse.

The gospel assumes this dilemma. It's a response to a hopeless situation—our inability to fix ourselves and resolve our separation from God's family. Frankly, this is what separates *biblical* Christianity from any other religion. The gospel of Jesus Christ says we are irretrievably lost in our sins and estranged from our heavenly Father, who desperately loves us. So God sent his Son, Jesus, "to seek and to save the lost" (Luke 19:10). Some religions deny human sinfulness and the accompanying idea that dealing with our sinfulness is necessary to be reconciled to God. Other religions acknowledge our sin problem but teach that the solution is human performance—repeating rituals, saying prayers, observing religious days, or otherwise being good enough to earn God's favor. These are lies.

Only the gospel of Jesus Christ is honest about the human situation and our inability to do a thing about it. It offers this singular truth: God had to provide the solution to remedy our estrangement from him, because none of us can fix the problem. Only Jesus can bridge the gap between us and God's presence, where we truly belong (John 3:16). The gospel tells the truth about us even though it's painful. It offers the love of God instead of lying to us or letting our self-deception go unchallenged.

## THE INDISPENSABLE ONE

*Stranger Things* reinforces the reality of what the gospel assumes and provides. It subtly reminds us that Christ is the *only* way of salvation (John 14:6). We're as lost as Will Byers, but the situation is even worse than that. Will couldn't solve his own predicament, and neither can we. We cannot defeat death; neither could Will.

We might be tempted to think that Will's situation wasn't hopeless. After all, his friends and his mom never gave up on him. That's true—but the fact is, they couldn't save him. Human tenacity didn't rescue Will; it took a "paranormal" power. What saved him was the *Stranger Things* version of supernatural intervention: Eleven.

This might sound overstated, but it's easily demonstrated when we ask ourselves a simple question: What happens if we remove Eleven from the story? How was Will saved? We might answer that it was through the efforts of his mom and Hopper. Yes, they find him in the climax of season 1. But how did they know where he was? *Eleven*. We might also credit Dustin, Mike, and Lucas. After all, without them, Joyce and Hopper wouldn't have known that there was a way to find Will. What was that way? *Eleven*. And why did the boys keep looking for Will after the body surfaced? Why did they believe he was still alive? *Eleven*.

The bottom line is that it was Eleven who told the boys about the Upside Down. It was Eleven who contacted Will in front of the boys in the AV clubroom through the shortwave radio. It was Eleven who confirmed for Joyce and Hopper in the makeshift sensory deprivation pool in the gym that Will was alive. It was Eleven who lured the Demogorgon to the gym by killing the soldiers threatening the boys, drawing it there with their blood. It was Eleven who made sure the Demogorgon wouldn't return to the Upside Down when Hopper and Joyce were on the verge of finding Will.

The truth is that without Eleven Will would have died. His friends would have abandoned the quest and his mom would have had no means to find him before it was too late. Only a power beyond normal human ability could save him. Remove Eleven, and the key elements to find Will would disappear and the means to save him evaporate. Similarly, remove the grace of God shown to us through what Jesus did on the cross, and salvation is no more—indeed, it's impossible. Jesus made precisely this point. Against the backdrop of his imminent betrayal and death, Jesus told his disciples not to let their hearts be troubled. They would be together again in his Father's house (John 14:1–2). When Thomas pleaded, "Lord, we do not know where you are going. How can we know the way?" Jesus replied with the one indispensable truth they all needed to fix in their hearts: "I am the way, and the truth, and the life. No one comes to the Father except through me" (John 14:5–6).

## IMPERMANENT FIXES

In addition to the characters of Hopper and Eleven, the theme of human inability to fix ourselves is made evident in other ways in *Stranger Things*.

Think about the emotional and psychological wounds and voids in the lives of other characters. They consciously (or unconsciously) seek healing and security in their relationships, but relationships are hard. They can be damaged and fail. Wounded people can never fix themselves through other wounded people. Co-dependency isn't a lasting solution; it's a fragile Band-Aid.

Take Nancy as an example. She's the high school girl we all remember. Hoping to escape her brainy-but-boring reputation, she gains identity through her boyfriend, Steve Harrington—who, at least at the beginning, wants only one thing from her. Nancy later confesses to Jonathan that she doesn't believe her parents ever actually loved each other. Their marriage, in her eyes, was one of economic convenience. It's for that reason she doesn't want life in a small town. Jonathan encourages her desire for independence, but when he later suggests that her tryst with Steve was about her wanting "to be someone else" besides herself, she takes offense.

He's right, of course. Murray, the paranoid investigative journalist hired to solve the disappearance of Barb, later observes the same insecurity in Nancy: "probably, like everyone, afraid of what would happen if you accepted yourself for who you really are and retreated back to the safety of Steve." Nancy is relentlessly plagued by guilt over Barb's horrible fate.

Instead of coming clean about what she knows of that night to her mom or the authorities, she decides to fix things herself (with Jonathan), a decision that contributes to the situation spiraling out of control.

Jonathan perceives Nancy's identity struggle clearly because he cares nothing for the expectations of his peers. He has his own issues, again deftly summarized by Murray when Nancy and Jonathan have to spend the night at his apartment: "Trust issues, am I right? Something to do with your dad." Jonathan tries to fix himself by withdrawing. He grows up in emotional isolation. He later plays the role of surrogate father, doing what he can to replace his loser of a dad (Lonnie) who walked out on his mom, Jonathan, and Will. When his brother vanishes, Jonathan can't help but shoulder the blame for not being home when it happened.

The members of the Party learn that relationships are hard, too. As tight as they are, the entrance of Eleven into their lives creates conflict. Lucas notices early on the way that Mike is looking at her and resents his friend being emotionally drawn away from the intimacy of their circle. After Will's funeral, when Eleven shows them that Will is alive, they instinctively conclude they must find the opening to the Upside Down to rescue him. Eleven fears the Gate, located in the lab that had been her prison, and intentionally leads them in circles away from the opening by mentally manipulating Dustin's compass. Enraged, Lucas calls her a traitor and suggests "maybe she's the monster," an insult that leads to a fistfight with Mike. Eleven uses her powers to stop it and renders Lucas unconscious. Efforts to fix everything on their own put the Party in danger of disintegration.

The Party is threatened again in season 2 by two related developments. A new character, Maxine "Mad Max" Mayfield unintentionally creates conflict between the boys. The sullen, cynical, red-haired Max is introduced as a new student in Hawkins Middle School, having just moved to Indiana from California. The boys are fascinated by her video game prowess and skateboard skills. They soon draw her into their group, and Lucas and Dustin begin to compete for her attention. The friendly rivalry isn't what creates tension, though. Conflict arises when Dustin discovers Dart, a pollywog that later transforms into a Demodog. The odd creature drives a wedge in the Party, as Mike and Will suspect it's from the Upside Down. Dustin and Lucas are inclined to tell Max what really happened to Will a year ago to explain Mike's insistence on excluding her from conversations about Dart. Even after Dart grows legs right in front of them, making it clear that Mike and Will's suspicion about the creature being a mini-Demogorgon is correct, Dustin protects Dart from Mike's attempt to smash him. Ultimately, Dustin's disloyalty to the Party has terrible consequences.

The experiences of these other characters—from Nancy to Jonathan to the Party—illustrate the same truth that is evident from the stories of Hopper and Eleven: the problems faced by the characters are otherworldly and beyond their abilities to solve. No matter their intentions and relationship bonds, the characters cannot save Will or Hawkins from the lethal threats that emerge from the Upside Down, the realm of death and evil. In fact, the heroes are not only inadequate but often make things more difficult. Hopper learns this the hard way: he comes to realize that Eleven is many things, but she isn't Sara. He must let her be who she is, and do what only she can do, if they are to be saved. The lesson is hard but essential. God made us in his image. Because we are God's imagers we share his attribute of free will. That means God has bound himself to allowing us to make our own choices rather than dictating those choices for us. But we are less than God, lacking his perfect nature. We are incapable of bridging that gap between ourselves and God. Instead of moving toward perfection, humanity transitions from one black hole to the next—creating dystopia, not utopia.

## THE RIGHT-SIDE UP

In *Stranger Things* we learn that paranormal problems require a paranormal solution. Eleven was that solution—the *only* solution. She alone can save Will, her friends, and everyone else from the realm of death, its demonic overlord, and his demonic servants. Likewise, our spiritual dilemma has but a single resolution. A supernatural problem requires a supernatural solution from the heavenly realm. This is the message of the gospel of Jesus Christ. Only he can reconcile us to God. Only he can save us from death and everlasting separation from God's family.

Yet so many people have and will continue to reject God's good news. Many do so because of the suffering and evil they've seen or experienced. They cannot fathom that the gospel is more powerful than evil and pain. But it is, and *Stranger Things* has something to teach us in that regard as well.

# MOMMA WANTS
# TO TALK

# HELP FROM BEYOND

**G**ood storytelling requires a handful of simple but crucial elements. One of those is a compelling villain. *Stranger Things* offers several, each one propelling the story line in different but related ways. The paranormal threats get most of the attention and capture viewers' imaginations. But sometimes things that appear the most ordinary are the most lethal. As memorable as the Demogorgon, the Demodogs, and the Mind Flayer are, a human evil is ultimately responsible for the freakish horrors. The human heart is capable of unthinkable treachery, often because its intentions are masked by unthreatening facades.

## DR. DEPRAVITY

In the story of *Stranger Things*, human depravity is best personified by the sinister Dr. Martin Brenner, the research scientist who heads Hawkins lab. Several things make Brenner skin-crawlingly creepy. For one, he clearly has no regard for human life. He doesn't blink an eye when cold-as-ice Connie Frazier puts a bullet into Benny's head after Brenner and his security detail arrive at Benny's restaurant to capture Eleven, whom they view as their property since they have raised the girl at the lab since infancy. Brenner speaks in a soothing monotone, his words whispered in grandfatherly cadence, his gentle eyes concealing a calculating mind and a deceitful heart. That

Brenner would later send Agent Frazier to Mr. Clarke's house in a ruse about a statewide AV club aimed at "recruiting" Mike, Lucas, and Dustin suggests that the lives of mere boys are of no consequence to him. Eleven herself puts her finger to her head in a shooting gesture to communicate to Mike just what kind of trouble they are in. She knows all too well—she saw Benny's murder while hiding in his kitchen.

One of the show's flashbacks to Eleven's past is especially illuminating, both into Brenner's dark nature and Eleven's abusive childhood. While at the lab, Eleven had been tasked by Brenner to kill a cat with her telekinetic powers. After she refuses, we see the scientist's two assistants haul Eleven to solitary confinement. Armed with cattle prods (which they apparently had used against children, judging by yet another of Eleven's flashback memories, this time with her "sister," Kali), they drag her toward her cell as she screams for compassion from "Papa." In a burst of anger she kills the two men with her mind. Brenner dispassionately steps past their bodies, his expression informing us that their deaths produce only experimental insight, not remorse. They are expendable. He touches Eleven's face tenderly, but he has no real compassion for her. As unfolding events reveal more clearly, his care for Eleven extends no further than her usefulness to his research.

## SCIENTIFIC ATROCITIES

It doesn't take viewers long to learn that Brenner has a long history of abuse connected to human experimentation. The most disturbing revelation is the truth behind the catatonic Terry Ives, Eleven's mother. In season 1 Joyce and Hopper go in search of her, not realizing just who she is. We see the pitiful, incapacitated woman staring blankly at the TV in her living room mumbling the same words over and over again: "Breathe ... sunflower ...

three to the right ... four to the left ... rainbow ... 450." We eventually learn that each element derives from some chapter in her tragic fate, from having Eleven stolen (literally) out of her womb by Brenner in the delivery room to her failed attempt to take justice into her own hands at the lab to the whereabouts of her little girl. The most chilling is "450"—the electroshock voltage setting ordered by Brenner, who watched indifferently as she was lobotomized.

Hopper first learns about Terry Ives while doing research in the town library, where he stumbles upon a picture of Brenner in a newspaper story about MK-ULTRA, a mind-control project. As some readers will know, MK-ULTRA is neither a fiction nor a conspiracy theory.[1] *Stranger Things* skillfully appropriates this classic but sordid saga of a government agency operating secretly within its own superstructure, circumventing the law and the nation's highest elected officials.

MK-ULTRA was officially approved by CIA director Allen Dulles in 1953. The program was conducted under a top-secret classification and ran possibly as long as 1973. Its purpose was to study the effect of drugs (e.g., LSD) and physical torture on the mind, with a goal toward mind control. The project became public knowledge in 1975 when it was exposed during congressional investigations into illegal CIA activities in both the United States and abroad (the Rockefeller Commission and the Church Committee).

It was ultimately revealed that the CIA was conducting several subprojects, including one known as MK-ULTRA subproject 58. It is this project that seems to be the point of focus for *Stranger Things*, as the focus of that subproject was experiments

---

1. See the CIA's online archive: https://www.cia.gov/library/readingroom/search/site/mk%20ultra.

in psychopharmacology to enhance psychic capabilities in its subjects.[2]

## EVIL BEGETS EVIL

While the plot of the series is framed by both paranormal and human evil, the depravity of Brenner and his associates are core to the storytelling. Hawkins lab is the epicenter of what's threatening the town and everyone in it. It's no surprise that the lab scenes were filmed at a former psychiatric hospital.[3]

Careful attention to the details of the plot bears this out. Eleven's terror at being forced to contact the Demogorgon in the Upside Down is what precipitated the tear ("opened the Gate") between the human world and the Upside Down. Dire consequences ensued: the appearance of the Demogorgon, the presence of the Shadow Monster, and the spawning of the Demodogs. While season 1 focused on Will's abduction, the collateral damage caused by the preternatural powers that passed through the Gate included the deaths of a few dozen lab workers and security guards, Barb, Bob Newby, and seven unnamed townspeople (by Brenner's count). Had Eleven not been Brenner's guinea pig, none of these terrible things would have happened.

But the crimes of Hawkins lab extend beyond the cosmic evil unleashed in the wake of Brenner's hubris. Brenner and his agents are responsible for the more mundane mayhem we

---

2. An excellent introduction to the American government's interest in and funding of psychic research is Annie Jacobsen's book *Phenomena: The Secret History of the U.S. Government's Investigations into Extrasensory Perception and Psychokinesis* (Little, Brown and Company, 2017). For a specific history of government mind-control research, I recommend Dominic Streatfeild, *Brainwash: The Secret History of Mind Control* (Thomas Dunne Books, 2007).

3. Matt and Ross Duffer, Shawn Levy, and Gina McIntyre, *Stranger Things: Worlds Turned Upside Down* (New York: Del Rey, Melcher Media, 2018), 61.

see play out in *Stranger Things*. They make Benny's murder look like a suicide. They ensure their own hirelings retrieve the faked body of Will. They send the town's coroner home and commandeer the autopsy. They bug the Byers and Wheeler homes before eventually ransacking them. They remove Barb's car and stage a runaway explanation for her disappearance. Even after Brenner's demise in season 1, the staff at Hawkins lab secretly records sessions between Will, Joyce, Hopper, and Dr. Owens. They also refuse to let Hopper or anyone else know about their futile efforts to keep the creeping rot of the Upside Down from further penetrating the town.

## AUTONOMY IS REBELLION

Ultimately, it doesn't matter that the otherworldly consequences of Brenner's research agenda were unintended. His delusion of moral autonomy and pursuit of secret knowledge unleashed hell in Hawkins. Pain, loss, and suffering ripple through the town to souls never known to Brenner and who would not recognize his name. Sin always harms in ways that are unforeseen, and the harm is genuine.

These truisms are scattered throughout Scripture. Numbers 32:23 warns its readers, "Be sure your sin will find you out." The apostle James was even more direct: "Desire when it has conceived gives birth to sin, and sin when it is fully grown brings forth death" (Jas 1:15). The human condition—the invariability and inevitability of death and our estrangement from God— was brought about from the very beginning by imperfections in human nature. Many Bible readers presume Adam and Eve were created perfect. They weren't. The standard for perfection is God. Adam and Eve were the *image* of God, the *likeness* of God (Gen 1:26–27); they were not God. God shared his attributes with them (intelligence, self-awareness, creativity); they did not possess such abilities exhaustively and perfectly like God does. In a nutshell, they were *lesser* beings.

One consequence of this lesser status was the lack of God's perfect nature. Adam and Eve could, and did, sin. They failed. Instead of obeying the will of their Father, they sought their own way. They wanted autonomy. Seduced by the serpent's suggestion that if they disobeyed God they would be enlightened, knowing things that only those in the supernatural realm already knew, they ate the forbidden fruit. The result was the entrance of death into God's good world and expulsion from God's home. While it's true they could not foresee all that their transgression meant for themselves, the human race, and creation at large, they were guilty. As the biblical epic proceeds through the book of Genesis and beyond, humanity doesn't get any better (Gen 6:5). Whether we like it or not, we're no exception to the trend. All of us go astray and seek the autonomy of our own way (Isa 53:6). None of us seeks God above our own desires (Rom 3:10–12).

## PROVIDENCE WINS

Something else should strike a familiar chord with Christians: evil can be thwarted by God and made to serve plans for the salvation and blessing of his human children.

Scripture makes it clear that, in the unseen hands of an all-powerful, loving God, sin and its consequences (unintended or otherwise) can be turned to deliverance and joy. While the human heart is "deceitful above all things, and desperately sick" as the prophet Jeremiah observed (Jer 17:9), God is still at work on our behalf. The Bible is filled with stories where God turned human evil to good, both out of mercy and as part of his plan to redeem his lost human children.

Perhaps the best example is what happened to Joseph (Gen 37–50). The eleventh of twelve sons of Jacob (whose name God changed to "Israel"), Joseph was favored by his father and, in turn, hated by his brothers (Gen 37:3–4), so much so that they secretly sold him into slavery. To cover their crime, they deceived their father into thinking he had been killed by an animal (Gen 37:18–33). Joseph wound up in Egypt. At first things went well (as well as they could in the context of being the property of someone else), but eventually Joseph was framed for a crime and sent to prison (Gen 39). Incredibly, the Bible says that God blessed Joseph for his believing loyalty to him. Eventually, by interpreting Pharaoh's dreams and saving Egypt from famine, Joseph was freed and elevated by Pharaoh to the second-highest position in Egypt (Gen 40–41). Things came full circle when his brothers showed up in Egypt to buy food. They did not recognize Joseph, but he knew them immediately. Rather than repay them with vengeance, Joseph saved his brothers and their families from starvation (Gen 42–47). But after their father died, Joseph's brothers feared revenge. Joseph's response is one we should all commit to memory:

> As for you, you meant evil against me, but God meant it for good, to bring it about that many people should be kept alive, as they are today. So do not fear; I will provide for you and your little ones. (Gen 50:20–21)

The entire tale of Joseph is thus one of God's providence. God took horrific evil, willingly perpetrated on an innocent man, and saved multitudes by turning it to good. God was still at work despite tragedy. Human depravity is no match for his power and wisdom.

We witness a similar triumph of good over evil several times in *Stranger Things*. The show portrays this resolution as a series of random, serendipitous events, not in terms of the operations of a good God. But the analogies are striking.

Toward the end of season 1, Hopper makes a deal with the folks in charge of Hawkins lab: he will tell them where Eleven is if they release him and Joyce, leave the boys alone, and forget about what happened in the wake of Will's abduction. All he wants is the chance to enter the Upside Down to save Will. Some fans of the show have seen this as a pure betrayal, a "Judas moment." I disagree. It's more akin to a "Sophie's choice" decision, where a person is forced to choose one of two tragic, unavoidable options to avoid an even more tragic outcome.[4]

Hopper isn't trying to betray Eleven; rather, he's trying to save Will and rescue Joyce from the terrible grief he knows all too well. He also doesn't want the boys harmed. Given his knowledge of Brenner, what Hopper does is reprehensible, but he has no other bargaining chip. But what happens in the wake of Hopper's decision is an example of unforeseen providence that *Stranger Things* communicates clearly despite not crediting God. Eleven defeats Brenner's armed force, thereby drawing the Demogorgon to the gym and away from Will, allowing Hopper and Joyce to save the boy.

---

4. *Sophie's Choice* is a novel by William Styron (1979), later made into a motion picture. It is frequently used as an example of a moral dilemma. As the Stanford Encyclopedia of Philosophy summarizes, "Sophie and her two children are at a Nazi concentration camp. A guard confronts Sophie and tells her that one of her children will be allowed to live and one will be killed. But it is Sophie who must decide which child will be killed. Sophie can prevent the death of either of her children, but only by condemning the other to be killed. The guard makes the situation even more excruciating by informing Sophie that if she chooses neither, then both will be killed. With this added factor, Sophie has a morally compelling reason to choose one of her children." *The Stanford Encyclopedia of Philosophy*, s.v. "Moral Dilemmas," by Terrance McConnell, Fall 2018 edition, https://plato.stanford.edu/archives/fall2018/entries/moral-dilemmas/.

Two similar instances come to mind, both from season 2. One of the more memorable subplots in the season is Dustin's discovery of Dart. Upon seeing Dart after Dustin brings him to school, Will has a flashback to the stomach-churning scene at the foreboding end of season 1. Alone in the bathroom one month after his rescue, Will vomits the same sort of creature into the sink, precipitating an Upside Down flashback. Will tells Mike that he believes Dart is from the Upside Down and, together, they try to convince the others. Dustin won't hear of it, claiming, "We have a bond." After Dart molts legs and makes the resemblance to the Demogorgon even clearer, Dustin protects the creature from Mike's attempt to kill it. Dart scampers away but is later found by Dustin, who secretly protects him, a violation of the Party trust that has deadly consequences.

Dustin's self-interested choice, even at the risk of the Party, illustrates the flaw in all God's human creatures: the desire for autonomy instead of accountability. Yet this terrible choice—this sin as it were—ultimately ensures the salvation of the Party. In an effort to help Eleven and Hopper get to the Gate, the Party, along with Steve, sets on fire the underground hub where the Demodogs feed, drawing the creatures away from the lab. During their retreat back to the surface, they are confronted by a Demodog, which turns out to be Dart. The beast's memory of Dustin is awakened by an offer of a Three Musketeers candy bar, which Dart eagerly consumes, allowing everyone to escape. Had Dustin and Dart not bonded, some or all of them would have been killed.

Another illustration of how evil is turned to good extends from Eleven's runaway hiatus in Chicago with Kali, another victim of Brenner, and her misfit friends. Eleven locates her mother, Terry Ives, who is able to alert the girl through blinking lights that "momma wants to talk." It is during Eleven's visit to the Upside Down to communicate with her mother that she learns what happened to her under Brenner's abuse. She also sees Kali, her older "lab sister" at Hawkins. Eleven is convinced that Momma wanted to talk specifically to lead her to Kali.

Once Eleven finds Kali, the older girl tries to convince Eleven to seek revenge, to channel her anger to develop her powers. When Eleven asks if Kali and her friends hurt and kill the "bad men," Kali tells her that "we make them pay for their crimes." Eleven affirms she has killed before, but these instances were in self-defense. In the end, Eleven refuses to kill Raymond, the man she knows lobotomized her mother at Brenner's instruction.

Eleven's resistance to the seduction of revenge is a watershed moment. She refuses to succumb to the dark side of her abilities. That Raymond, the intended victim, has two small children—both of whom were in his apartment when Eleven, Kali, and the rest of their gang show up—helps tip the scales in favor of mercy. Afterward, Kali is angry but softens toward Eleven. Her protest—"Were we not also children?"—fails to convince Eleven that killing Raymond is just. After all, Eleven knows what it's like to lose a parent.

In the end, the episode produces clarity for Eleven about the course of her life and her search for identity. Her powers cannot change the past, but they can avert more disaster. She decides to return to Hawkins to save her friends. Ironically (or providentially, for our analogy), Kali's advice to use anger to amplify her power enables Eleven to defeat the Shadow Monster. When the Shadow Monster attacks her, she focuses on evil done to her and her mother and overcomes the assault, closing the Gate.

## THE RIGHT-SIDE UP

These vignettes from *Stranger Things* illustrate fundamental truths of the gospel of Jesus Christ. God's love isn't thwarted by depravity; quite the opposite. God's love is so powerful that it will not only heal the wounds we suffer at the hands of depraved people but will subvert their evil intentions. But we will only experience the fact that God's love outlasts depravity by trusting him. That's hard, to say the least, just as it must have been unimaginably bewildering for the disciples of Jesus to witness his humiliating crucifixion. The gospel accounts tell us clearly that they had no idea what its point was and expected anything but a resurrection (Matt 16:22–23; Mark 9:10–11; Luke 24:36–49). God meant it for good.

So it is with evil in our lives. It is certainly true that no evil any of us have experienced is new in this fallen world. It is equally true that people who have suffered the very things that now course through your mind as you read these words have emerged from their ordeals with stronger faith. But all of that is academic posturing until you experience it firsthand. I personally know people who endured years of physical, psychological, and sexual abuse or who were homeless and lost in addiction who are now powerful agents of God's love to others. But I also know their stories. God's transformation and judgment of the evil done to them took time. Each one would testify, though, that it was a mistake to think that God was not present in their suffering or that God was only acting in overtly dramatic events that could not be missed. Invariably, though, God was present moment by moment in the arduous, day-to-day labor of recovery. It's much harder to see the unseen hand. It takes eyes of faith to see the workings of God, but they are there, often visible only in hindsight.

# NOBODY
# IS NORMAL

# THE GIFT OF UNIQUENESS

Season 1 of *Stranger Things* ends at Christmastime. The Demogorgon conquered, Will is alive but, as we learn before the finale closes, not well. Nevertheless, he's at home where he belongs. But it's a painful time for others. Since he never met her, Will doesn't feel the anguish that the rest of the Party, especially Mike, must endure in the wake of losing Eleven.

It is ironic that the loss of the boys' savior is set on the cusp of Christmas, the time Christians everywhere celebrate the Advent of the Savior of the world, Jesus Christ, the Son of God. Christmas is the time God became man, born as a baby, utterly dependent and helpless, brought into the world under the disinterested gaze of livestock. His young childhood was spent in exile from his home, a refugee from Herod. He would grow up under Roman tyranny in obscurity and relative poverty. Here was God among humankind, hidden in plain sight.

Even more astonishing than his circumstances is that God chose this course. As Paul writes, Jesus "did not count equality with God a thing to be grasped, but emptied himself, by taking the form of a servant, being born in the likeness of men. And being found in human form, he humbled himself by becoming obedient to the point of death, even death on a cross" (Phil 2:6–8). Incredibly, the Son of God knew from the very beginning that creating humanity would come with a high cost to himself—and he willingly accepted it.

## LOOKS ARE DECEIVING

No figure in history was more than he appeared to be than Jesus. He looked completely normal but was anything but. Surely there must have been clues. In the first several centuries after the New Testament Gospels were written, writers speculated about what Jesus did as a boy. These ancient literary works, called "infancy gospels" by scholars, certainly are interesting. These texts allege that Jesus could talk while an infant (he told his mother, Mary, that he was the Son of God); his birth clothes were fire repellent; he brought clay animals and birds to life; and a leper even was cleansed with the baby's bathwater. Sounds like a kid who didn't need to be occupied but certainly needed to be watched.

The New Testament Gospels contain none of these stories about Jesus. The only event from his infancy that any of them record is his family's escape from Herod's murderous panic into Egypt and their subsequent return after the king's death (Matt 2:13–15). From that point forward to his adulthood the Gospels offer only one biographical detail about Jesus: the incident when his parents lost track of him and found him in the temple asking astonishing questions of the teachers (Luke 2:42–51). When Joseph and Mary found him and asked him why he had treated them so badly, Jesus tellingly replies, "Why were you looking for me? Did you not know that I must be in my Father's house?" (Luke 2:49). Beyond that episode, Matthew, Mark, Luke, and John give us the impression that there was nothing of importance to report. Jesus was just like everybody else ... except that he wasn't. Remind you of Eleven?

## THE WEIRDO ON MAPLE STREET

I mentioned earlier that the first episode of the show ends with Mike, Dustin, and Lucas encountering the drenched, forlorn Eleven out in the woods. It didn't take a genius IQ to see that she was lost and possibly homeless. The boys have a choice to make based entirely on appearances. As is true throughout the show, Mike emerges as the leader. Unbeknownst to his parents, he had rallied the Party together to search for Will. It's obvious that they're not supposed to be running around alone at night, even under normal circumstances. This night is far from ordinary. It's been only twenty-four hours since Will's disappearance, an alarming event that Chief Hopper suspects is no juvenile charade. The boys know that taking the girl to adults means getting in some serious trouble at home. So Mike makes the entirely predictable, impulsive decision to take her to his house on Maple Street, planning to have her "accidentally" show up the next day when his mom is home. She will know what to do.

Eleven's behavior among the group immediately gives every indication she's a stranger in a strange land, a visitor to a foreign time and place. The boys pepper her with questions: Do you have a phone number to call your parents? What happened to your hair? Did you have cancer? Are you in trouble? She's so unresponsive that Dustin claps in her face to see if she's deaf. When Mike gives her some dry clothing, she thinks nothing of shedding the only thing she's wearing, the oversized T-shirt from Benny. The boys freak out and stop her. Mike has to instruct her about "privacy," a concept with which she apparently has no familiarity. He tries to shut the bathroom door for her, but she stops him. He figures out immediately that she's frightened of small, closed spaces. We learn why later.

Dustin and Lucas are quick to decide that Eleven is "mental," concluding she escaped the "nut house" in the neighboring county. Her puzzling behavior is the context for the episode's title: "The Weirdo on Maple Street." Viewers know even at this early stage that Eleven isn't a weirdo. There's far more to her than meets the eye. The short, fateful time at Benny's Burgers told us that much. Annoyed with the fan at the diner, Eleven stalled its motor with her mind while no one was looking. Her shorn head, gaunt frame, and vulnerable expression perfectly disguise the power and resolve that dwell within her.

The paradox of Eleven reminds us of other unlikely fictional heroes. In the contemporary pop culture canon, one thinks immediately of Yoda ("Judge me by my size, do you?"), Frodo Baggins (hobbits are called Halflings for a reason), and Harry Potter (a David to Voldemort's Goliath). But this is more than a literary trope. Some of the most famous names we know reached the heights for which they are known despite daunting circumstances. J. K. Rowling was a single mom living on government welfare. Oprah Winfrey was born into deep poverty in rural Mississippi. Henry Ford went broke five times before he founded the Ford Motor Company. Walt Disney lost a job early in his career after his boss told him that he "lacked imagination and had no good ideas." Both literature and history are filled with people who, defying expectations, were far more than they seemed.

## SCARY BUT GOOD

Eleven's presence in the show—call it her advent—parallels Jesus' in certain ways. A few Christian bloggers have seen cryptic Christology in Mike's nickname for Eleven ("El").[1] The name "El" is, as Bible students will know, one of the Hebrew names for

---

1. Examples include Relevant Magazine's blog (https://relevantmaga-zine.com/culture/gospel-according-stranger-things/) and the Church Life Journal blog (https://churchlife.nd.edu/2017/12/15/welcoming-stranger -things-without-baptizing-them-too/).

God.[2] It is also a common noun for a deity in ancient languages similar to Hebrew.

Some of these parallels may be coincidental. In the Bible Israel was (corporately) God's "son" (Exod 4:22). The prophet Hosea's words, "Out of Egypt I called my son" (Hos 11:1), are a reference to Israel's escape from Egypt in the exodus. The Gospel writer Matthew sees an analogy to Jesus' escape as a child out of Egypt back to Nazareth and quotes Hosea's statement to highlight the association between the individual and corporate Son of God. With this in mind, add that Michael is Israel's guardian prince in the Old Testament (Dan 10:21; 12:1). In *Stranger Things* Mike at times plays the role of El's caretaker, and he is certainly her defender throughout the show. Is this supposed to whisper the relationship of Michael to Israel and Israel's Messiah?

These points of overlap are interesting but speculative. They require intentional thinking on the part of the show's creators. As I noted in the introduction to this book, I don't think that was really happening much if at all. I think a more rewarding (and occasionally humorous) way to look at Eleven's role is to process some of the interactions between Eleven and the boys in the Party in comparison to Jesus, his disciples, and others who witnessed his miracles.

The boys are confronted with Eleven's "otherness" in a scene from the show's second episode. While in Mike's room, Eleven chances upon a picture of the boys, one that includes Will. Her happy expression morphs into transparent apprehension as she slowly points at the missing boy's face. Mike understands that she's seen Will, but where? How? Later, with Lucas and Dustin present, the boys try in vain to get answers. Eleven

---

2. For instance, Gen 14:18, 22; Isa 40:18, where the Hebrew term translated "God" is *el*.

telekinetically slams the room's door shut after Lucas threatens to tell Mike's mom about her. Her powers exposed, blood running from her nose, her answer is clear and commanding: "No." The boys are intimidated, to say the least.

Interesting to note, then, that on more than one occasion, Jesus' acts of power draw a response of fear, not delight. When Jesus healed the paralyzed man, we're told that "when the crowds saw it, they were afraid" (Matt 9:8), and "fear seized them all" (Luke 7:16). The response of the people who knew the demon-possessed man of the Gerasenes was fear: "Then people went out to see what had happened, and they came to Jesus and found the man from whom the demons had gone, sitting at the feet of Jesus, clothed and in his right mind, and they were afraid. ... Then all the people of the surrounding country of the Gerasenes asked him to depart from them, for they were seized with great fear" (Luke 8:35–37).

Though initially alarmed at Eleven's abilities, the boys are soon drawn in. Their exchanges with her turn to humor and elation. Dustin tries to get Eleven to use her powers to make Mike's model of the Millennium Falcon fly. But Eleven isn't interested in entertaining them. (She does make the model fly later, when she's alone and bored out of her skull.) Jesus wasn't a performer either (Matt 12:38–39; 16:1–4).

At the conclusion of a more ominous scene, Dustin is exultant when Eleven, after spectacularly halting Mike's plunge into Sattler Quarry in midair and then levitating him back to safety, makes quick work of the two bullies whose threats forced the boy into the suicidal plummet: "Yeah, that's right! You *better* run! She's our friend, and she's *crazy*! You come back here and she'll kill you!" Jesus didn't use his power to punish his enemies, but I still have to think some of the disciples would have wanted to see Jesus knock them down a peg or two. I know if I had been one of the disciples, I would have begun every day hoping to see Jesus do something amazing, especially if he embarrassed his critics. It's a very human impulse to want to see the extraordinary—and to have bullies put in their place.

The disciples also got frustrated with Jesus or were not content with what he taught them. There were times when they wanted to know what he was doing or why he wasn't doing something they expected. They wanted to know why he was teaching in parables (Mark 4:10; 7:17). Why not use clear language? Not satisfied with Jesus' comments about divorce and remarriage, "the disciples asked him again about this matter" (Mark 10:10). Sometimes they were hesitant to ask him for explanations (Luke 9:45; John 16:16–20).

The boys of the Party certainly get annoyed with Eleven. Once it is revealed that Eleven knows how to get to Will (through the Gate), they insist on being led to the Gate. Eleven, afraid of the place, intentionally messes with their compasses to lead them astray. Jesus also used misdirection when it served his purposes (John 7:1–10).

In one of the show's most memorable scenes, the boys try to protect Eleven from the "bad men" of Hawkins lab. Their efforts to get Eleven to safety by bike is short-lived, as they are soon cornered by several vans from the lab. That Eleven can take care of herself is reinforced when she flips one of the vans into the path of the others. Similarly, Peter impetuously tries to violently protect Jesus from the soldiers who come to the garden of Gethsemane to arrest him (John 18:1–11). But the Son of God does not need nor want assistance: "Shall I not drink the cup that the Father has given me?" (John 18:11).

Let's face it. If we discovered that we had a friend who had otherworldly powers, the result would be both apprehension and excitement. *Stranger Things* captures the blend of emotion well, as do the Gospel writers, who are honest with their readers about the effect Jesus had on people.

## WANTING TO FIT IN

By the end of season 1, what we really learn from Eleven's advent is that, while she is the savior of her friends and the town of Hawkins, she desperately wants to be normal. We can see it early on, in the scene in Mike's room before she recognizes Will. Her heart is warmed by Mike's friendship with the boys. As time goes on, she learns what friends are and how they treat each other. "Friends don't lie" is arguably the most iconic line from the show. She yearns to be included. She covets the bond that the Party shares. Watching Eleven balance her desire to bond with the others while securing their safety and fighting her fears, we wish we were in the Party as well.

There are other scenes that convey her longing to be like her friends. When Eleven wanders into Nancy's room, she is captivated by pictures of her baby sister, birthday cakes, and friends. It's all foreign to her, which makes it easy to see how much she wants it. When her distortion of the compasses is interpreted by Lucas as sabotage and disloyalty and he angrily suggests she's more of a monster than the Demogorgon, Mike and Lucas get into a fight. Eleven intervenes and sends Lucas flying through the air, knocking him out cold. She runs away from Mike and Dustin while they try to revive Lucas. We next see her at a pond, where she puts on the wig the boys had found for her. She wants to be pretty, but she's once again an outcast. In despair she screams and sends shockwaves through the water.

Her longing for normalcy is present in every episode in season 2. She yearns to see Mike and the rest of her friends. She aches at the loss of her mother, a pain that turns to anger when she discovers her true fate. Eleven wants to fit in. She wants a family. She wants friends. She wants to love and be loved. These simplest of human desires are the cry of her heart.

Yet other characters in *Stranger Things* don't describe being normal as something to covet. Jonathan gives voice to this sentiment in season 2. When Will gets angry about being called "Zombie Boy" at school and being treated like a baby at home, Jonathan cleverly agrees that he's a freak—and that's a good thing. He asks Will, "Do you want to be normal? Do you want to be just like everyone else?" He then drives his point home: "Nobody normal ever accomplished anything meaningful in this world." Will should capitalize on his gifts and use them to the fullest for lasting value and accomplishment.

Eleven's wish to be normal and Jonathan's sage observation are not at odds. Both sentiments are true and compatible. There's no hint that Eleven believes the absence of her powers would mean being reunited with her friends. Her powers are not the obstacle. She sees their value clearly in her exchange with Kali before returning to Hawkins. After Kali insists to Eleven that her friends cannot save her, that they cannot help her heal, Eleven replies: "No, but I can save them." Eleven isn't trying to change to be accepted; she wants to be accepted for who she is. Mike and the rest of the Party can give her that.

## THE RIGHT-SIDE UP

It takes time for Eleven to realize that her otherness is a gift. The love and loyalty of her friends are part of that as is their mission against enemies held in common. Jesus knew his heavenly Father loved him, and he had a clear sense of mission. By the time he was twelve, he knew who he was and what his purpose was. Jesus expressed the two thoughts poignantly: "For this reason the Father loves me, because I lay down my life that I may take it up again" (John 10:17).

Nevertheless, Jesus didn't run around calling himself the Messiah, the anointed one. Instead, his favorite self-reference was "son of man." This descriptive phrase can point to his deity in certain contexts, but most often it simply means "human one." We have to admit that it's a bit odd for a guy to refer to himself as "the human one."

My take on this quirky fact in the Gospels is that Jesus enjoyed being human—being "normal" by earthly standards. He felt no shame in being a human (Heb 2:11). My favorite Christmas carol, "Hark the Herald Angels Sing," expresses it beautifully: Jesus was "pleased as man with man to dwell." He also enjoyed the people who believed in him—the ones whom God "gave him out of the world" (John 17:6). He prayed to God, his Father, "I desire that they also, whom you have given me, may be with me where I am, to see my glory" (John 17:24).

For the town of Hawkins, thankfully someone was not normal on Maple Street. The rest of us can say the same thing of the One born in Bethlehem so long ago. Both of them showed up just when they were needed to do precisely what only they could do.

# 6

## "NO MORE"

# THE COST OF SACRIFICE

T he climactic scene of Eleven's self-sacrificing defeat of the Demogorgon in the school science room is one of the most iconic moments in *Stranger Things*. The showdown between the show's paranormal points of opposition was not unexpected. Further, I was struck immediately by the Christian imagery and import: the Christ figure surrenders her life to defeat supernatural evil and save those whom she loves.

In the preceding chapter we observed how the muted arrival of the Son of God into the human world marked the beginning of God's salvation plan coming full circle. Christ's arrival among people on the social periphery was the beginning of a long journey, one that would be marked by both personal suffering and spectacular miracles and that would end in heart-wrenching loss. So it would be with Eleven. Her own appearance was likewise known to very few kids, the least of Hawkins's residents. The boys learn not only about Eleven's powers but also her trauma. They witness firsthand what she's capable of, as well as the cost of her intervention on their behalf.

We might think that, for those who consider themselves Christian, these elements would be unmistakable. After all, the incarnation of the Son of God and the story of the cross are the core of the Christian faith. But despite the coming and work of Christ on our behalf, many Christians today don't seem to understand the gospel.

I don't make that statement lightly. It's a conclusion to which I've been dragged, kicking and screaming, over my forty years of being a Christian. It's a simple thing to tell the gospel story and say that we join God's family by believing it—by putting our full faith and trust in what Jesus did on the cross on our behalf. But many Christians, while embracing this notion intellectually, struggle mightily when it comes to surrendering to its simplicity.

By now some readers are wondering what I'm talking about. Others will understand precisely because they have either come through that struggle or are currently experiencing it in real time. I understand. I had to fight the same fight.

## WHAT IS THE GOSPEL?

It's fairly easy to define what the term "gospel" means. We did that in this book's introduction. It's the "good news" about how Jesus' death, burial, and resurrection are the basis for God's forgiving of our sins, making us acceptable to himself, and giving us everlasting life in his family. In the language of traditional theology, it's the good news that the Son of God became a man, suffered and died on the cross so that our sins would no longer keep us out of God's family, and rose from the dead so that we could also overcome death and be with his Father, our Father, the only true God, forever. The apostle Paul called putting our trust in this gospel "the obedience of faith":

> Paul, a servant of Christ Jesus, called to be an apostle, set apart for the gospel of God ... concerning his Son, who was descended from David according to the flesh and was declared to be the Son of God in power according to the Spirit of holiness by his resurrection from the dead, Jesus Christ our Lord, through whom we have received

grace and apostleship to bring about the obedience of
faith. (Rom 1:1–5)

It's worth considering what Paul *didn't* say in his explanation. There's nothing in that passage (or any other verse in
the Bible) defining the gospel as "the obedience of perfection."
That's because the content of the gospel is not about what we've
done, or might do, or need to do. It's about what was done, on
our behalf, by someone else—namely, Jesus. That's good news
for all of us, because none of us is perfect. But *we have to be made
acceptable to God.* The gospel tells us how that happens.

The passage also doesn't say anything about "the obedience
of comprehension." We may not understand how things like
God becoming a man or rising from the dead work. We may not
understand much theology at all. God doesn't ask that we get
a comprehensive education before we believe. He wants us to
embrace fully a simple idea: that we cannot save ourselves, but
what Jesus did can save us. What happened on the cross is what
God will accept, and nothing else.

This helps us understand Paul's description of the gospel as
"the obedience of *faith*." What God wants is our full trust that he
will honor his solution to our spiritual dilemma. That means we
aren't to put our trust in our moral behavior, a religious ritual, or
our sincerity. The content of the gospel is God's offer to forgive
us and give us a permanent place in his family based on what
Jesus did, not on anything we do.

Put another way, the genuine, biblical gospel cares *only* about
who you already are. You are human. That means you are the
object of God's love and plan from the very beginning. None of
that requires performance. It just *is.* God loved us "while we
were still sinners" (Rom 5:8). That's why the gospel is good news:
we are lost without it.

To be blunt, the gospel doesn't let us take any credit. We need to remember—and put our full trust in their genuine, conclusive finality—the last words Jesus said on the cross: "It is finished" (John 19:30).

## ENOUGH

The climactic scene of Eleven's self-sacrificing defeat of the Demogorgon in the school science room captures these words of Jesus perfectly—even verbally. The parallel is so explicit that it is easy to conclude that it's one of the rare instances in the show that deliberately emulates the story of Jesus. At the very least, it is powerfully providential.

Fans of the show will recall the events that lead to the scene. Immediately after dispensing with the small army threatening her and her friends inside Hawkins Middle School, Eleven falls unconscious. Before the boys can move her, Brenner shows up with a handful of security guards, who grab the boys from behind when they challenge him. Brenner pulls Eleven to a sitting position. She momentarily regains enough of her faculties to recognize his face. He tells her he's going to take her back home, "so we can make all of this better; so that no one else gets hurt." Looking at him, she groans "bad ... bad" and reaches out for Mike. Before Brenner steals her away, the Demogorgon, drawn by the bloody scene of Eleven's demolition of Brenner's soldiers, smashes through the gym wall. The soldiers release the boys and in unison turn their weapons on the beast.

As chaos ensues, Dustin carries the stricken Eleven to the science room as fast as he can and places her on one of the lab tables. With emergency lights punctuating the darkness, the boys listen to the rapid spurts of gunfire in the hall while Mike tries to comfort Eleven, and himself, with promises of the future. Silence breaks through the din, prompting Dustin to stutter,

"Is he ... is he dead?" The lull in weapon fire is only temporary. Before anyone can hope out loud, the Demogorgon shatters the door. Panicking, the boys frantically (and pointlessly) feed Lucas rocks for his wrist rocket. They have just witnessed hundreds of rounds of live ammunition fail to take it down—but to their stunned amazement, one of Lucas's projectiles propels the creature backward, pinning it to the wall.

Of course, Lucas's aim isn't what drives the creature into this upright, prone position. It's Eleven. Off the table, she strides resolutely past the boys toward the Demogorgon, now bound by the invisible force emanating from Eleven's mind, its sinewy arms outstretched against the blackboard in cruciform profile, writhing in anger. Shouting "Eleven, stop!" Mike runs toward her. It is his Malchus moment: like Peter's ill-conceived severing of the high priest's servant's ear in order to protect Jesus (John 18:10), this cannot stand. Replacing the stricken man's ear (Luke 22:51), Jesus repudiates the deed: "Do you think that I cannot appeal to my Father, and he will at once send me more than twelve legions of angels? But how then should the Scriptures be fulfilled, that it must be so?" (Matt 26:53–54). What will happen *must* happen. And so Eleven thrusts Mike away from her, sending him flying into the cabinets at the back of the room.

Now standing before the Demogorgon, the personification of death, she looks back at the boys, last of all Mike, to whom she calmly bids goodbye. She lingers for a moment, sharing his tearful gaze. Turning again to the monster, she glares at it and whispers, "No more." Spending the rest of her power, her scream mingling with that of the creature's in an ear-splitting crescendo, she dematerializes the Demogorgon to the black ash of the otherworldly abode of death from which it came, vanishing with it. It is no coincidence that the episode transitions to Hopper and Joyce saving Will. Death has been conquered, enabling the two to arrive in time to revive Will and save him. They will soon learn, as the boys already know, that Eleven's sacrifice saved them all.

## REFLECTION

"No more." "It is finished."

And it really is. It's time for people seeking a genuine relationship with God to discover that such a relationship has nothing to do with us convincing God to love us. He always has.

In the course of my own Christian experience and ministry I've discovered that Christians actually struggle with this. This is why I suggested above that I get the impression that Christians don't really grasp the gospel. They are caught in a performance trap, but salvation cannot be earned. They struggle with the gospel. Inside the mind and heart of many Christians, the notion that just believing what Jesus did for you just doesn't seem right. Surely we have to *do* something. How else could we deserve it?

The biblical truth is that we don't deserve what God offers in the gospel, and that stirs internal conflict. It feels wrong to get something so wonderful without having done something to deserve it, even just a little—which makes us feel guilty. This guilt distorts our ability to see the gospel as the unconditional gift it is.

Reversing the curse of death and bringing his estranged children back into his family forever was something only God could do. So he did, through the work of his Son. This is why Jesus is who he is and did what he did. All God asks is that we trust in what he did and nothing else. It is indeed finished.

# 7
## NEVER THE SAME

## FINDING HOPE AMID CHANGE

O ver the forty years of my Christian life I've noticed a tendency in how the story of Jesus is told. Given the centrality of what happened on the cross and the ensuing resurrection for the Christian faith, it's no surprise that those events get a great deal of attention in preaching. As a result, relatively little attention is directed to the period between those two events. That omission in focus means missing something—something that *Stranger Things* manages to capture and convey very well.

Think about the circumstances of the gospel story. The death and resurrection of Jesus occurred barely three days apart. Jesus had prepared the disciples for what was going to occur. Sometimes he did this cryptically, warning them, "Just as Jonah was three days and three nights in the belly of the great fish, so will the Son of Man be three days and three nights in the heart of the earth" (Matt 12:40). Another Gospel writer informs us that Jesus also could be blunt about what to expect: "He began to teach them that the Son of Man must suffer many things and be rejected by the elders and the chief priests and the scribes and be killed, and after three days rise again. And he said this plainly" (Mark 8:31–32). In this instance, what he said was so clear that "Peter took him aside and began to rebuke him" (Mark 8:32). Peter was hearing the words of Jesus clearly. He just didn't like what he was hearing.

Perhaps resistance to what Jesus told them can explain other passages that have the disciples utterly flummoxed by the resurrection. Consider what occurred a short time after the empty tomb was discovered:

As they were talking about these things, Jesus himself stood among them, and said to them, "Peace to you!" But they were startled and frightened and thought they saw a spirit. And he said to them, "Why are you troubled, and why do doubts arise in your hearts? See my hands and my feet, that it is I myself. Touch me, and see. For a spirit does not have flesh and bones as you see that I have." And when he had said this, he showed them his hands and his feet. And while they still disbelieved for joy and were marveling, he said to them, "Have you anything here to eat?" They gave him a piece of broiled fish, and he took it and ate before them. (Luke 24:36–43)

Luke's account gives us the impression that after the crucifixion the disciples weren't looking for a resurrection. When Jesus died they may have remembered what he said but evidently didn't take it seriously enough to expect it to happen. They were stunned. So great was their doubt that, in the same episode, Jesus had to "[open] their minds to understand the Scriptures" (Luke 24:45).

The point is a simple one: the last thing in the minds of Jesus' followers was that he would be back from the dead. Instead we catch glimpses of disillusioned men who had resigned themselves to the ignominious end of a man they had been far too gullible in following.

Peter's decision to go back to his trade after the death of Jesus tells us exactly where the disciples stood psychologically ("I am going fishing"; John 21:3). Six other disciples decide to join Peter—at least two of which are never described in the New Testament as being fishermen (John 21:1–2). These men are directionless and defeated.

There's something else less obvious lurking in the background. In the wake of what had happened to Jesus, the disciples *needed* to disappear. After their time of very public exposure, Jesus' disciples had better blend in. Doing so would keep them out of harm's way. Going back to their lives before Jesus would signal that the rivalry to Judaism's authorities (and by fateful extension, Rome) would not resurface. The disciples had seen the error of their ways. They had been disabused of their naivete. They would be no threat in the future and wished to stay clear of further recriminations.

The days between the cross and the resurrection, then, weren't filled with breathless anticipation of the return of Jesus. Instead they were filled with despair and trepidation. If you had bumped into one of Jesus' followers shortly after the crucifixion, there would have been no talk of hope or mission. Life would never be the same. They had forsaken everything to follow Jesus, and now he was dead. They had been all in. Now it was all over. Of course once Jesus had risen and shown himself to them, *life would never be the same* for altogether different reasons.

## EVERYTHING'S THE SAME, JUST DIFFERENT

While *Stranger Things* has its own chronology that has no intention of following that of the gospel story, the second season of the show is framed in these same terms.

The initial episode of season 2 sets the tone that life would never be the same because all was lost and there were good reasons to be fearful. The music subconsciously creates this atmosphere. Oingo Boingo's "Just Another Day" plays in the background as Hopper pulls up to the police station and finds Murray, whom he disdains as a conspiracy theorist, waiting for him. It's musical subversion. It really *isn't* just another day. When his secretary rings him to investigate contamination in Merrill's pumpkin patch, giving him an excuse to get away from Murray, he isn't headed for another small-town peacekeeping mission. The creeping contagion at Merrill's farm awakens him to the fact that, almost a year later, Hawkins is *not* the same.

When the season opens, we learn that Mike has remained inconsolable over the loss of Eleven. He's been counting the days since his last sight of her. His hope that she will make contact again is dying. His sense of despair is palpable. The other members of the Party are fearful of government retaliation. This is most clearly telegraphed by Lucas when he divulges to Max what really happened the previous year in Hawkins. His paranoia that she won't take the revelation seriously is informed, to say the least. And then there's the mystery of their friend Will's unexplainable, involuntary trances.

The new reality therefore takes the form of sadness and dread in the Byers house throughout season 2. As Will's mysterious condition becomes more evident, Joyce's anguish and anxiety for her son grow. Hopper tries in vain to comfort her: "Nothing is gonna go back to being the way it was, not really. But it'll get better. In time." But does he believe himself? Something is (literally) rotten in Hawkins and the contamination is spreading. The first episode of season 2 had ended with the revelation that Eleven is living with Hopper in a family cabin known only to him. Concealing her has him on constant edge.

As was the case in season 1, the sense of looming doom extends from both a human and a supernatural source. Despite Brenner's absence, it doesn't take long for us to distrust the new personnel at Hawkins lab. Will goes to the lab with his mom and Hopper for a medical checkup from its new head, Dr. Owens.[1] The ostensibly innocent appointment is being secretly recorded. Afterward, Dr. Owens's assistant informs him, "They're ready for you, sir." Viewers thus learn very early that Owens and the rest of his new cohorts know far more about what's happening in Hawkins than they are willing to divulge.

The audience eventually learns that the people at the lab are also looking for answers. It's hardly comforting when even the bad guys are afraid. During the appointment, Will tells Dr. Owens about his vision of the Shadow Monster—one seen by viewers in the first few minutes of season 2. Will's interpretation of its meaning sets the tone: the evil didn't want to kill him ... just everyone else. Owens is, in fact, the least of the town's worries.

Season 2 of *Stranger Things* thus captures the mood of the post-crucifixion context. For the boys of the Party, their savior, Eleven, is dead. The loss is crushing and leaves them vulnerable to present dangers, some more detectable than others. It's not a happy setting. But viewers already sense that Eleven will be reunited with her friends to protect them and handle unfinished business at the lab. She is more than a one-time deliverer from the Demogorgon. She has even greater supernatural evils to confront. The groundwork is being laid for the *Stranger Things* version of ongoing spiritual warfare.

## CHANGE FOR THE BETTER

But life would never be the same in Hawkins for another, better reason. Eleven would—and indeed has—returned from the Vale

---

1. In a casting master-stroke, Owens is played by Paul Reiser, whom eighties science-fiction fans will never forget as the smarmy and treacherous Burke in Ridley Scott's *Aliens*, a franchise from which *Stranger Things* repeatedly draws.

of Shadows. Her escape from the realm of the dead is laced with resurrection imagery.

This might be hard to see, since we as viewers never see Eleven die. We know she entered the Upside Down having dispatched the Demogorgon. We also see Hopper leave her food in the woods at the end of season 2, leading us to believe she's not entirely gone. It's also difficult since, as Christians, we tend to think of resurrection as only the reanimation of a corpse. That idea is certainly put forth in the resurrection accounts in the Gospels and certain New Testament letters. However, resurrection can be conceived as re-materialization, the re-assemblage of no-longer-extant remains into bodily form. This alternative conception was necessary for obvious reasons. Bodies were lost at sea, eaten by animals, or consumed by fire. If corpses were not embalmed, they turned to dust. There's no corpse to reanimate in such circumstances.

Readers will recall that Eleven disintegrated into the Vale of Shadows along with the Demogorgon in the climactic science-room scene of season 1. The moment is vividly replayed in a flashback that opens the second episode of season 2. Eleven awakens whole in the Upside Down's counterpart to the science room. Since the beast is no more, viewers must assume that Eleven's reconstitution is the result of her own power. No other character dematerializes in the normal, common world when entering the Upside Down. We see something similar happen in the ethereal Upside Down when Eleven "sees" people by tapping into it, but this scene transcends those portrayals. What Eleven does here is unique.

After waking Eleven sits up, fresh blood streaming from her nose. Staggering into the hallway, she first tearfully then frantically calls for Mike. The familiar gurgling rumble of the Upside

Down draws her attention. Peering through a hole at the center of the paw print on the wall at the end of the hall (the same entry point into the school used by the Demogorgon in the finale of season 1), she sees the police outside Mike's house. Inside, the Wheelers' home is crawling with federal agents. The entire sequence takes place a very short time after her destruction of the Demogorgon. Eleven uses her powers to widen the hole and reenters Hawkins Middle School on the other side. She goes to Mike's house and cautiously observes his interrogation from outside the window. For a fleeting moment, Mike wonders if he's seen her. Alerted by his expression, the agents stream out into the night searching for her. We see her hiding under a log in the woods and crying before the scene gives way to the present time, roughly a year later.

Flashbacks to the days following the end of season 1 punctuate episodes of season 2, filling in other details. Eleven must survive alone in the woods. By now her hair has grown out. She kills a squirrel with her kinetic powers, hurling the rodent headfirst into a tree. While cooking her meal over an open fire, she's discovered by a hunter, whom she knocks cold with a piece of firewood before taking his coat. In still another flashback Eleven chances upon the box in which Hopper has placed a Tupperware container of food and some Eggo waffles, which viewers see him do a month after Will's rescue, at the end of season 1. Her expression reveals her surprise. She looks around for who might have left it before taking the food and running away. Sometime later Eleven surveils the box and discovers her benefactor is Hopper. She follows him after the food drop and reveals herself to him. It is at this point that Hopper takes her in, harboring her in his grandfather's cabin.

## THE RIGHT-SIDE UP

For the disciples, the resurrection appearances of Jesus transformed the new, fearful normal into a new hope. This hope had been foreshadowed by Jesus, but they never understood his words clearly. The hope that Eleven would also emerge from the realm of the dead was also foreshadowed, at least for viewers, by Hopper's secret food offering. And it is at precisely this point that *Stranger Things* is most visually connected with Christian teaching.

Fans of the show have drawn attention to the shape of the box in the woods in which Hopper places a meal for Eleven: its shape conforms precisely to an ordinary communion host container found in many Catholic churches. Further, Eggos are round like communion wafers. The show is not consciously communicating theology here. After all, it is Eleven, the Christ figure, sustained by the offering (the food). Nevertheless, the imagery connects Eleven to Jesus.

The Eggo offering is emblematic of Hopper's hope. This idea becomes more poignant when we later see that Eleven is the literal and emotional surrogate for Sara, Hopper's lost little girl. Eleven is also the hope for Mike, the Party, the rest of the characters, and the clueless townspeople of Hawkins. It's a hope that, barely over a year before in the town's history, didn't exist. Truly Eleven is both the occasion and the proof that nothing will ever be the same.

Hopper's gesture thus communicates a promise that will sustain viewers in season 2—that darkness will not win the day—and reminds Christians of the same truth on a much grander scale. The hope of the gospel is grounded in the resurrection. God has "caused us to be born again to a living hope through the resurrection of Jesus Christ from the dead" (1 Pet 1:3). As Paul said, "If Christ has not been raised, your faith is futile and you are still in your sins" (1 Cor 15:17). When we trust the gospel, nothing will ever be the same.

# 8
## NOT A
## NORMAL FAMILY

# BOUND TOGETHER BY CAUSE

**E**very family suffers conflict, struggle, and loss. How family members respond to these things determines whether the bonds survive and sustain or deteriorate and unravel. The former confirms our sense of who we are and what we can or should do in life. The latter outcome can devastate our self-image and the course of our lives.

## FAMILY IDENTITY

Family is at the heart of *Stranger Things*. Whether because of biology, sense of personal loss, or shared experience, bonds of trust unite and propel the characters. Family defines identity and purpose in life in crucial ways.

The Byers family is a case in point. By the end of season 1, each member—Will, Jonathan, and Joyce—have gone to the *Stranger Things* version of hell and back. The three emerged from their trials more tight-knit than ever, but their experiences redefined their identities. They're still family, but now they have secrets to guard: what really happened to Will, the reality of the Upside Down, what went on at Hawkins lab, and what they know about that girl with the shaved head. The same goes for the other major characters in *Stranger Things*. Hawkins is now home to a small fellowship united by a common ordeal, a tiny band whose knowledge and experiences make them different from everyone else.

Season 2 injects new characters into this mix. One of the most important is Bob Newby, Joyce's romantic interest. Bob is a native son of Hawkins whose obscure claim to fame is that it was he who started the middle-school AV Club. Nicknamed "Bob the Brain" in high school and owner of a Radio Shack franchise in town, Bob is an adult nerd, a grown-up version of our heroes in the Party. At one point early in season 2, the good-hearted geek-entrepreneur suggests that he, Joyce, and the boys move out of Hawkins. Joyce's reply is more honest than Bob can fathom: "This is not a normal family." Bob naively replies, "It can be."

What has made the Byers family "not normal"? Exposure to genuine paranormal realities. Will and his mom understand that there is a world beyond the one they have known and experienced. So does Jonathan, Will's brother. He rescued Nancy from the Upside Down portal in the woods. He battled the Demogorgon inside his own house. Joyce both communicated with Will across the barrier between two worlds and saw into the Upside Down. She witnessed Eleven's power to penetrate the Upside Down with her mind. No, they're not a normal family.

## THE FAMILY OF GOD

The gospel does the same thing for those who grasp its truth and experience the forgiveness of God's love, shown to us through the cross. The apostle Paul articulated the point well: "Therefore, if anyone is in Christ, he is a new creation. The old has passed away; behold, the new has come" (2 Cor 5:17). Believers have a new identity. They are different because of a genuine spiritual encounter with God through Jesus Christ.

The New Testament articulates this new reality in startling ways. The apostle John writes in a letter, "See what kind of love the Father has given to us, that we should be called children of God; and so we are" (1 John 3:1). The thought echoes something he had written in his Gospel account of Jesus' ministry: "To all who did receive him, who believed in his name, he gave the right to become children of God" (John 1:12). We are part of God's family. We were given that status not by any natural birth or our own pursuit but by the power of God (John 1:13). We are siblings of Jesus (Rom 8:29; Heb 2:11).

The family of God is certainly not a normal family. Christians share an identity that transcends the normalcy of this world. The very term "Christian" identifies us with Christ. We are not of this world precisely because Jesus was not of this world (John 17:14, 16). Christian, do you know who you are? Just as importantly, do you see your brothers and sisters in Christ for who they truly are?

As mentioned in this book's introduction, God's intention in creating humanity was to make them part of his family. God didn't decide to create humanity because he lacked something. His perfection means he wasn't incomplete without us. He wasn't lonely. If our creation wasn't meant to meet some deficiency in God, we can only conclude that God wanted humans to be with him, to enjoy them, and to see their joy at being part of his family. This makes good sense if we recall that Eden was God's home—it was where heaven came to earth. Humans belonged with God. They were created fit for God's presence.

The fall ruined this. Humanity became estranged from their Father as a result of rebellion. What should have been normal— life with God—became impossible. This is why God himself had to remedy the problem. And so the eternal Son became a man to remedy death and be the basis of forgiveness of sin. Death can be overcome by resurrection, and one cannot have resurrection without death first. Only an eternal being that becomes vulnerable to death can provide an eternal solution. That's the only way the math adds up.

To participate in this resurrection, one must be fused to, made part of, Christ. Various metaphors are used in the New Testament to describe this status for all who embrace the gospel. Believers are "in Christ": "in Christ Jesus you are all sons of God, through faith" (Gal 3:26). We become the "body of Christ" (1 Cor 12:27). We have been "united" with Christ (Rom 6:5). We "have put on Christ" (Gal 3:27). The family of God is spectacularly supernatural. It is made possible only through God's divine power.

## COMMON CAUSE

Exposure to otherworldly places and powers not only redefines identity for the heroes of *Stranger Things*; it also instills them with new, unified resolve. Their shared trauma, brought about by their contact with the Upside Down and its denizens, endows them with a sense of mission. This begins with the Byers family in their pursuit of Will. Hopper soon follows in the quest once he confirms Brenner's conspiratorial efforts to mask Will's disappearance as an accidental death. He and the boys of the Party become privy to the paranormal reality at the heart of the mystery though Eleven. Working together they locate and rescue Will. But less than a year later they all discover that the supernatural threat to the entire town has expanded exponentially. They must act to save each other—and Hawkins.

These dynamics become evident in the flow of the show's first two seasons. Insight into the reality of the Upside Down begins with Joyce. Her faith that Will is alive is unquenchable. Even after Hopper brings her news of the body and despite her visit to the morgue to identify Will, she tenaciously believes the impossible. She has experienced a spiritual reality (Will's communication through her phone and the Christmas lights) that she cannot understand. None of it corresponds to a reality she can comprehend. What she has experienced is completely irrational, but she knows it's real and won't be convinced otherwise.

Joyce is an evangelist of sorts within her circle in Hawkins. She's the irresistible force in the lives of Jonathan and Hopper convincing them that Will is alive. Though Nancy caught a glimpse of the Demogorgon when she returned to the scene of Barb's disappearance, it is Jonathan who has the answer to Nancy's uncertainty about what she saw. Together they experience the parallel dimension touching their own world. Eleven plays the same role for the boys of the Party. Through her they learn that Will is indeed alive, though not present in their familiar plane of reality. The truth spreads one person at a time, expanding the group of believers.

Eventually the players working separately to find Will join forces. Comparing notes, they devise a plan to locate Will. Eleven must overcome her fear of the sensory deprivation tank. Its use heightened her power, allowing her to penetrate deeper into the Upside Down. In turn it led to the rift in space and time, opening the Gate through which all their troubles had come. Jonathan and Nancy decide to draw the Demogorgon away from Will with their blood, a plan that would have ended tragically without Steve's timely appearance at the Byers house. Hopper and Joyce take just as dramatic a risk by breaking into the Hawkins lab compound. Getting caught was part of Hopper's plan to surrender Eleven for the sake of Will and the boys.

In season 2 we see more of the cooperative sense of mission, particularly in the last two episodes. They must all pull together to deceive the Shadow Monster. Tearing the Byers' shed apart, they create a chamber that prevents the invisible Mind enslaving Will from learning their whereabouts. Joyce, Jonathan, and Mike break through to Will past the intelligence possessing the boy by reminding him of earlier childhood memories. Will taps Morse code messages with his finger. Hopper relays the tapping. The boys decipher the dots and dashes. Nancy writes down the letters: "CLOSE GATE." It's a total team effort. Jonathan and Nancy, who earlier exposed Hawkins lab, join with Joyce to exorcise the Shadow Monster from Will. "Babysitter" Steve and the boys set fire to the tunnel hub, drawing the Demodogs away from the lab so that Eleven and Hopper can get to the Gate. Hopper protects Eleven, who is battling the Shadow Monster, by picking off the Demodogs trying to reach her.

While it's true that Eleven is ultimately the indispensable element to conquering the Shadow, if we think more deeply, we'll notice that disunity would have undermined the entire effort. Success required mutual trust and faith in each person to do their part and to resist the temptation of self-interest at the expense of the others. What if Nancy and Jonathan had parted ways after their tiff in the woods? Would they have discovered the Upside Down? If not, their crucial insight that the Demogorgon was drawn by blood would have been lost. What if Lucas had not rejoined the Party after his fight with Mike over Eleven? It was Lucas who spotted the vans leaving the lab, alerting the boys to get Eleven out of the house. What if Steve had just chosen to stay out of things to distance himself from Nancy in self-pity? Since he repeatedly saves the boys with Max in season 2, it's hard to underestimate his significance.

## ONE BODY

Sadly, life teaches us that this sort of single-minded devotion to a cause—shunning personal status, pride, and ambition for the good of everyone—isn't normal. Jesus knew that. On the very night of his betrayal, he prayed for unity among his disciples and others who would come to believe in him: "Father, keep them in your name, which you have given me, that they may be one, even as we are one" (John 17:11).

The commitment of the *Stranger Things* characters to each other provides an important reminder for the body of Christ. Aside from sharing a common identity, all believers share a common mission. There is a reason we are in this present world, though many believers seem to be unaware of it or are perhaps distracted by the cares (or self-interests) of this life.

Think back to our earlier discussion of our creation by God. Our purpose for being in this world begins with representing God. This is the meaning of being created in God's image (Gen 1:26). The image of God isn't a quality put into us. To be human is to be God's image. The concept is more like a verb than a noun. God created humans as his imagers—his representatives or proxies on this earth. We image God when we imitate God, acting on his behalf, living as he would if he were embodied.

For Adam and Eve, the first of God's human children, imaging or representing God on earth meant stewarding creation (Gen 1:26). They were also tasked (along with their own children) with spreading over the earth, in effect making the rest of the world like Eden (Gen 1:28). God's plan was to have humans be his agents to make his world all he wanted it to be and to enjoy it with him. Doing that would mean treating everyone in ways consistent with what they were: siblings and partners.

Because we all enter the world estranged from God, we must be brought back into his family. That's the role of the gospel. God so loved the world that he sent his Son for that purpose (John 3:16). Bringing God's estranged children back into his family is the goal of representing him here. The gospel "is from God, who through Christ reconciled us to himself and gave us the ministry of reconciliation. ... We are ambassadors for Christ" (2 Cor 5:18, 20). This mission was handed down by Jesus when he went back to heaven after his resurrection (Matt 28:18–20; Acts 1:8). As I've written elsewhere:

> As evil had spread like a contagion through humanity after the failure of the first Eden, so the gospel spreads like an antidote through the same infected host. We are *carriers* of the truth about the God of gods, his love for *all* nations, and his unchanging desire to dwell with his family in the earthly home he has wanted since its creation. Eden *will* live again.[1]

## THE RIGHT-SIDE UP

Jesus never told his followers to do what he didn't do first. He gave his life to bring humanity back into God's family. He laid down his life for his siblings. We are to imitate him—to image him—in doing the same. This is why New Testament writers refer to Jesus as the image of the invisible God (Col 1:15) and the exact imprint of God (Heb 1:3). It's why the goal of the Christian life is being conformed to Jesus' image (Rom 8:29) and being transformed into his image (2 Cor 3:18).

Most of us don't give this much thought. Consequently, it's hard to think of how we might intentionally do this. The answer is simple: imitate Jesus, whether by speech or behavior. All of our relationships—personal, home, business, work, church—would be different if we consciously remembered who we are as imagers of God and that other people share that same status and need to be brought back into God's family.

---

1. Heiser, *Supernatural*, 166.

Every Christian has a role to play in someone else's life, whether they are outside the family of God or part of it. Sometimes that will come by intention; at other times it will come without knowing that's what's happening. Providence is always at work. We have all been gifted by the Holy Spirit for specific tasks needed for the health of the whole body. Paul's metaphor of the human body and its disparate parts is right on target. We all can't be doing the same thing. Our diversity is designed—and it's an asset, not a liability. Instead of coveting the task someone else is doing, we must discern our own gifts and apply them wherever we are for the work of God's kingdom.

This is not a normal way to think about life, especially in modern Western culture, where the individual is glorified. That's fine. We are not a normal family. And our mission is anything but ordinary. Because our identity and mission are so important, we can expect a struggle.

# WE KEEP GIVING IT WHAT IT WANTS

# THE BATTLE WITHIN

**M**any Christians lose sight of who they are and what it means to be children of the Most High God. This world is not our home. We will be raised with Christ after we leave this world because we are united to him. He is our brother. He became human so that humans could be made like Christ (1 John 3:1–3) who is the archetype—"firstfruits" in Paul's language—of resurrection (1 Cor 15:20–23). When we lose sight of our status and destiny, our sense of mission fails. If we do not grasp the significance and implications of who we are, we won't know what to do or how to do it.

Unfortunately, we have other problems. There are both internal and external spiritual obstacles to accomplishing God's purposes. He made us partners with him in bringing his children back home, but we are weak and vulnerable. We are weak in that we are embodied ("in flesh" as the Bible often describes us). That makes us susceptible to impulses and appetites that are distractions from our mission and which might be self-destructive. Externally, we are vulnerable to spiritual forces that actively seek our failure and ruin. In the next two chapters we'll consider these struggles in that order and see how *Stranger Things* provides vivid analogies for both.

## THE ENEMY WITHIN

In the final episode of season 2 our collective heroes are holed up in the Byers house trying to come up with a plan to save themselves and the town of Hawkins. They managed to circumvent the Shadow Monster's possession of Will long enough for the stricken boy to tell them they must close the Gate. When asked by Joyce if she can close the Gate, Eleven at first remains silent but then affirms she can close the Gate. Hopper protests. The following exchange ensues:

> ELEVEN: I can do it.
>
> HOPPER: You're not hearing me.
>
> ELEVEN: I'm hearing you. I can do it.
>
> MIKE: Even if El can, there's still another problem. If the brain dies, the body dies.
>
> MAX: I thought that was the whole point.
>
> MIKE: It is, but if we're really right about this ... I mean, if El closes the gate and kills the Mind Flayer's army. ...
>
> LUCAS: ... Will's a part of that army.
>
> MIKE: Closing the gate will kill him.

Alarmed, Joyce leads the group into Will's room. In the *Stranger Things* timeline, it's early November in Indiana, but the window to Will's room is nevertheless open. Glancing at the open window Joyce whispers, "He likes it cold. ... It's what Will kept saying to me. He likes it cold. We keep giving it what it wants." Nancy and Jonathan see her point immediately. They reply in tandem: "If this is a virus, and Will's the host, then ... we need to make the host uninhabitable."

As believers we face a struggle similar to Will's battle with the evil forces in *Stranger Things*. I'm not talking about demonic possession. Rather, Joyce's intuition transforms Will's possession by the Shadow Monster into a vivid metaphor for the Christian's struggle with the flesh.

In New Testament thought, "the flesh" generally represents a source of opposition to God. While "the flesh" often refers to the human body, the term includes immaterial struggles as well—thought patterns, attitudes, predilections, vanities that arise in the life of the mind. For the Christian, living "for the flesh" is to pursue life without regard to God's will, a life fixated on "the desires of the flesh and the desires of the eyes and pride of life" (1 John 2:16). Pursuit of the sins of the flesh is a death spiral that begins in the mind: "For to set the mind on the flesh is death, but to set the mind on the Spirit is life and peace. For the mind that is set on the flesh is hostile to God" (Rom 8:6–7).

In the New Testament the flesh is often and intentionally contrasted with the Holy Spirit, who indwells believers when they embrace the gospel (John 14:17; 2 Tim 1:14): "You, however, are not in the flesh but in the Spirit, if in fact the Spirit of God dwells in you. Anyone who does not have the Spirit of Christ does not belong to him" (Rom 8:9). Believers do not live "according to the flesh but according to the Spirit" (Rom 8:4).

It is important to remember that God's love for us is not predicated on behavior. The gospel is freely offered to us. Trusting in the grace of God is what brings salvation, not self-reformation or correct behavior. We become part of God's family when we *believe* the gospel. On our own we are lost (Luke 19:10), "alienated from the life of God" (Eph 4:18). God didn't wait until we cleaned up our act to love us. He loved us "while we were still sinners" (Rom 5:8).

## OUR MOTIVATION

As Christians, our lifestyle should confirm that we have aligned ourselves with Jesus and now follow him. This is what the Bible means by discipleship. Disciples seek to live like their master. They imitate their master. We imitate Jesus to show our love for him and for God. Jesus was the ultimate imager of God. As Jesus did what he did because he loved God, so must we.

Because we trust the message of the gospel, we should be moved to live in such a way that we are effective ambassadors for the gospel, showing others who aren't in the family of God what they are missing (2 Cor 5:18–20). Just as Jesus honored people by telling them the truth, blessing them in their time of need, and extending compassion to damaged souls, our own lives should convey that these are the things that steer our behavior—not self-gratification and considering ourselves more important than others. People will not see Jesus through our lives if we are driven by self-indulgence and an appetite for power and status—John's "the desires of the flesh and the desires of the eyes and pride of life."

## A PAINFUL NECESSITY

In the story of *Stranger Things*, Joyce similarly recognizes the need to fight against internal destruction. Until the scene where our small fellowship of "believers" is at its collective wits' end, Joyce had done what the thing inside her son demanded. We can hardly blame her for doing so initially. When she brought Will home, right after he had been taken over by the Shadow Monster in the schoolyard, she had no idea what she was dealing with. That all changed when she saw the entity within her son use the boy as a tool to entrap and kill most of the lab's staff. This horrific turn of events ultimately led to Bob Newby's gruesome death at the moment of their escape from the lab. Joyce wasn't going to let it have its way any longer. She knew that what needed to be done would be painful but absolutely necessary: "We need to burn it out of him."

The subsequent scenes of Will's exorcism are some of the most visceral in the show. Joyce, Jonathan, and Nancy must expose Will to intense heat. When the small boy breaks one of his bonds and seizes his mother's throat, squeezing the air from her lungs,

Nancy jabs him with a hot poker from the fire. Simultaneously, Steve sets fire to the underground hub. With one last convulsion, the Shadow Monster takes corporeal form and bursts out of Will, shattering the door of Hopper's cabin, roaring in fury as it streams back to the hellish Vale where it belongs.

By analogy, the life of discipleship can be painful. The early church understood that believers who refused to turn from sins that damaged the community and its witness to the world had to reap what they were sowing. To mention just one example, Paul told the Corinthian church to expel one of its members for sexual immorality (1 Cor 5:1–13). They were to "purge the evil person from among you" (1 Cor 5:13). The goal was redemptive: that the guilty would be forgiven (2 Cor 2:5–11). The man in question was to leave the community where God's presence dwelt among believers and remain out in the world, the domain of Satan. While the unrepentant offender would still be saved, his path would lead to self-destruction (1 Cor 5:5).[1]

Though arduous and agonizing, dealing with sin is necessary to spiritual health. To drive this point home, Jesus used extreme metaphors: "If your right eye causes you to sin, tear it out and throw it away. ... If your right hand causes you to sin, cut it off and throw it away. For it is better that you lose one of your members than that your whole body go into hell" (Matt 5:29–30). Jesus' point is echoed elsewhere in the New Testament. The "works of the flesh"—living in a way that violates God's moral laws for abundant life—result in self-destruction. What good comes out of giving the flesh what it wants?

> Now the works of the flesh are evident: sexual immorality, impurity, sensuality, idolatry, sorcery, enmity,

---

1. Compare 1 Cor 3:16–17; 6:19–20; 2 Cor 6:14–18.

strife, jealousy, fits of anger, rivalries, dissensions, divisions, envy, drunkenness, orgies, and things like these. (Gal 5:19–21)

Instead of "present your members to sin as instruments for unrighteousness" (Rom 6:13), we are to "put to death therefore what is earthly in you: sexual immorality, impurity, passion, evil desire, and covetousness, which is idolatry" (Col 3:5).

## THE RIGHT-SIDE UP

Each Christian is a redeemed child of God in a yet-to-be redeemed, resurrected, and glorified body. The flesh—our body and our formerly unredeemed ways of thinking and living—is in constant conflict with the soul (1 Pet 2:11). Rather than living and thinking like we did when we were alienated from God, oriented by self-gratification and what this life offers, the Bible teaches us to "walk by the Spirit" (Gal 5:16). The result will be the opposite of self-destruction. We will bless others and be blessed with the fruits of the Spirit, who indwells us (Gal 5:22–24).

Instead of giving our flesh what it wants, we must have what Paul calls "the mind of Christ." Jesus, the ultimate imager of God, showed us the way:

If there is any encouragement in Christ, any comfort from love, any participation in the Spirit, any affection and sympathy, complete my joy by being of the same mind, having the same love, being in full accord and of one mind. Do nothing from selfish ambition or conceit, but in humility count others more significant than yourselves. Let each of you look not only to his own interests, but also to the interests of others. Have this mind among yourselves, which is yours in Christ Jesus, who, though he was in the form of God, did not count equality with God a thing to be grasped, but emptied himself, by taking the form of a servant, being born in the likeness of men. And being found in human form, he humbled himself by becoming obedient to the point of death, even death on a cross. (Phil 2:1–8)

Our trust in the gospel and the security it gives—that we are acceptable to God and will live with him forever—are crucial for the abundant life God wants us to have (John 10:10). "The world is passing away along with its desires," John tells us, "but whoever does the will of God abides forever" (1 John 2:17). Our faith in God's grace will make us "strong in the Lord and in the strength of his might" (Eph 6:10). It's a good thing; we have serious supernatural enemies.

# THE HIVE MIND

10

# THE BATTLE AGAINST THE UNSEEN

**T**he characters and story line of *Stranger Things* provide analogies for truths that Christians need to grasp more fully (our identity and mission) and for impediments to living out the truth of the gospel (distractions of "the flesh"). Those problems arise from within. They are, in certain respects, caused, nurtured, and actualized by ourselves.

As challenging as it is to allow God's thoughts and ways to have preeminence over our desires and behavior, we have other problems. We are vulnerable to external spiritual forces that actively seek our failure and ruination. The hive mind of *Stranger Things*—the collective preternatural threat from the otherworldly Upside Down—is aptly analogous to the way the New Testament frames the supernatural opposition impeding the accomplishment of the believer's mission.

## THE POWERS OF DARKNESS

Many Christians have only a superficial understanding of the powers of darkness. Part of the problem is that we lack understanding of the Old Testament context for the Bible's depiction of these powers. Most believers frame the subject of supernatural evil only in light of the fall in Eden described in Genesis 3. But the fall was the first of three supernatural rebellions.[1] Failure to

---

1. For lengthy discussions of the biblical passages behind the points

grasp this point of the supernatural epic we call the Bible leads to flawed assumptions about supernatural evil.

A brief overview of the story of evil forces in the Bible will be necessary to help understand the full scope of their power and continued threat. Most people, whatever their religious affiliation, are familiar with the Bible's main supernatural adversary: the serpent, eventually referred to as the devil or Satan. But he was not the only malevolent figure in the spiritual world.

In the days before the flood a second mutiny erupted in God's heavenly realm. A cadre of God's celestial children defected from their heavenly home and assigned sphere of service, violating the boundary between heaven and earth (Gen 6:1–4; 2 Pet 2:4; Jude 6). In biblical days, the breach spawned the Nephilim giants and their kin, who are referred to as Anakim and Rephaim (Gen 6:4; Num 13:32–33; Deut 1:28–33; 2:1–3:11).

This crime would reverberate on earth in tragic ways. It led to bloody conflict between God's children and the clans of giants shortly following the exodus of Israel from Egypt. On the way to their landed inheritance, God forewarned Moses and Joshua about what awaited them. He told them that, while Esau's relatives had eradicated the bloodlines of the Nephilim in places like Moab and Ammon (Deut 2:8–22), they could still be found in Bashan (Deut 2:23–3:11) and Canaan (Num 13:22, 28, 32–33; Deut 9:1–2; Josh 11:21–22). God intentionally steered Israel into their strongholds. The giants had to be eliminated.

Joshua was eventually able to destroy most of these foes, though some escaped to places later known as the Philistine cities (Josh 14:12–15). It was from one of those cities, Gath, that

---

included in the sketch offered here, see my books *The Unseen Realm: Recovering the Supernatural Worldview of the Bible* (2015) and *Demons: What the Bible Really Says about the Powers of Darkness* (forthcoming).

Goliath would come. Only when David, a messianic archetype, and his men later killed Goliath did this particular shockwave from the supernatural rebellion of the sons of God run its course (1 Sam 17:23–49; 1 Chr 20:4–8).

The disembodied Anakim and Rephaim were thought to inhabit the realm of the dead.[2] On the basis of these and other biblical texts, Jews of the later Old Testament period through to Jesus' day taught that demons were the disembodied spirits of the dead giants. These were the demons we know from the Gospels. The reason the demons were labeled "unclean spirits" was their mixed origin (mixtures in Old Testament law were deemed abhorrent and unclean).

But a second, residual side effect of the supernatural breach lingered. (As *Stranger Things* shows us, a breach between worlds creates more than one problem!) Like the otherworldly contagion festering in Will Byers at the end of season 1, something unseen had happened to humanity as a result of the supernatural violation of the human dimension. Humanity had been corrupted because the fallen sons of God had transmitted forbidden knowledge that led to bloodshed, immorality, and idolatry, resulting in the proliferation of human depravity. This in turn is why the Old Testament forbade contact with the dead and attributed the dark arts to the disembodied spirits of the underworld (Deut 18:9–14; Lev 19:26–31; 20:6, 27). It's why Paul and Jude see false teaching as the legacy of "wandering spirits" and refer to what their opponents taught as the "teachings of demons" (1 Tim 4:1) leading to blasphemy and idolatry (Jude 6–10).

Following the supernatural rebellion of Genesis 6:1–4, it would be understandable if the main character of the biblical

---

2. In Isa 14:9 the Hebrew word *rephaim* has the meaning "shades," while in Prov 9:18 and Job 26:5 it refers to "the dead."

story—God—had decided to scrap the plan. The creation of humanity (not to mention his earlier supernatural children) looked like a terrible idea. But omniscient beings don't have bad ideas any more than an all-loving Father could totally destroy creatures he had made in his own image. After the first rebellion, God had expelled the rebels from his presence. After the second rebellion God sent the flood to wipe the slate clean, promising to never do so again (Gen 9:12-17). God did not forsake humanity—and while that was good news, it didn't prevent God's children from turning their backs on him again.

One more catastrophic celestial insurrection would play out early in the biblical story. After the flood God had reiterated to Noah and his family what he had told Adam and Eve—to have children and spread out over the earth (Gen 9:1). The goal had been to spread the goodness of Eden. Repeating the command telegraphed that God wanted to try again. But instead, God's earthly family congregated in one place, which would become known as Babel (Gen 11:1-9). They decided to build a ziggurat tower, historically part of a temple complex. They wanted God to come to them in the place of *their* choosing. That wasn't God's plan.

In response, God divided humanity by languages and geographical destiny. By doing so, God abandoned his earthly children, allotting them "according to the number of the sons of God" (Deut 32:8).[3] God assigned the rule of his human children to other members of his heavenly family. Humanity didn't want him as their king, so he obliged.

Over the course of time the Bible tells us that these sons of God became corrupt, enslaving and abusing their populations

---

3. The ESV translation has appropriately adopted the Dead Sea Scroll manuscript wording. See also Deut 4:19-20; 17:1-3; 29:23-36.

(Ps 82). These were the gods worshiped by the peoples of the earth. They would be the entities referred to in the Bible as the supernatural "princes" over nations (Dan 10:13, 20) and, later, as the principalities, powers, rulers, thrones, and authorities that opposed the spread of the gospel (Eph 3:10; 6:12; Col 1:16; 2:15). These cosmic adversaries are not the demons of the Gospels. Their power is far greater than harming people or turning them into puppets made of flesh. Their goals are far more ambitious. They sought, and still seek, world control. They are cast as having geopolitical dominion.

This overview of the evil forces in the Bible shows that the world contains an army of unseen sinister intelligences, guided by a superintelligent malevolence, collectively watching humanity through a thin preternatural veil, waiting for opportunities to dominate and decimate human lives. If you've seen *Stranger Things,* that should sound familiar.

## AN OTHERWORLDLY ARMY

At the end of season 1, the heroes of the series collectively played their roles against the evil threatening the unsuspecting town of Hawkins. Their efforts set the stage for Eleven to take down the Demogorgon with her otherworldly power. We're barely into season 2 when we realize the Party and the rest of the small band who know the truth are going to be tested again, this time by an even more malicious force. Early on we get our first glimpse of the Shadow Monster, the preeminent enemy from the Upside Down, through Will's terrifying "true sight" episode at the arcade. The intelligent, ethereal evil is also at work underground, spreading a putrefying contagion that is surreptitiously burrowing its way under the entire area.

The second and third episodes of season 2 introduce us to Dart, the pollywog creature discovered by Dustin in the trash can outside his home. We learn by virtue of Will's response, Mike's intuitive thinking, and the creature's own metamorphosis that the Upside Down is now home to a horde of violent, bloodthirsty beasts. Though smaller than the dreaded Demogorgon, they outnumber it exponentially.

At the end of the third episode the Shadow Monster takes possession of Will. Following Bob Newby's well-intentioned advice, the doomed boy tried in vain to resist the Shadow. In the Upside Down we see every pore of his small body penetrated by black, tentacular jet streams. On the other side, his mother tries to shake the catatonic Will back to consciousness. Standing stiff and erect, the whites of his eyes faintly visible at the bottom of his fluttering eyelids, the boy who had escaped the Upside Down was now under the power of its lord.

The fourth episode resumes the possession scene. After he regains consciousness, Will tries to explain to his mom what's happened to him. He can't remember the event, but he knows more than he ever has. His mind is filled with "now memories," what the Shadow Monster sees and thinks. Discovering that her son's temperature is below normal, Joyce decides to warm him in the bathtub. A foreign, menacing answer emanates from Will, whose body has become a shell for the Shadow Monster.

As the series moves on we discover that Will cannot resist the entity inside him. The boy is now a host, doing the bidding of the Shadow on the plane of reality opposite the Upside Down.

Will's inability to verbalize what's going on inside him gives Joyce an idea: "What if you didn't have to use words?" Perhaps Will can draw what he sees. He does, producing hundreds of sheets of apparently meaningless crayon etchings. Hopper and Joyce recognize they are like puzzle pieces and begin to assemble them. Hopper discerns that the tentacle-like "roads" aren't roads at all but tunnels. It's a fateful insight, one that nearly costs

Hopper his life. The chief finds the tunnel hub and is snared by the rotting limbs and vines, themselves conscious and alive, empowered by the Shadow Monster. Later, in another flash of insight, Bob realizes that Will has managed to draw a map of Hawkins. The intuition allows them to save Hopper's life but also sets in motion the series of events that put Joyce, Will, Hopper, Bob, and Mike in Hawkins lab, where the Shadow Monster induces Will to invade the lab, leading to Bob's tragic death.

In episode 5 we finally learn, through revelations of Dr. Owens at Hawkins lab, that the entirety of the underground contagion, the horde of Demodogs, and the Shadow Monster are metaphysically connected. In the words of Dustin and Mike, the Shadow Monster is a superorganism, the brain that controls the "hive mind" (akin to the Mind Flayer in D&D).

In episode 9 of season 2 we witness Joyce's revelation: "We keep giving it what it wants." It is in this precise moment that our heroes awaken to what must be done. The darkness is a hive mind, moving as one with a singular goal. *Are they capable of the same?* They must be a cohesive collective so that the hive mind can be distracted, fragmented. They each have small but indispensable roles—or else Eleven's supernatural power will be spent without success.

## KINGDOMS IN CONFLICT

The hive mind and the coordinated combat launched against it are a metaphor for spiritual warfare in *Stranger Things*. Unfortunately, clarity on how the New Testament frames spiritual warfare is lacking in many sectors of contemporary Christianity today. Spiritual warfare is not simply about shouting at demons or performing ritual acts to put them in their place. Spiritual warfare is fundamentally about the conflict between two kingdoms: the kingdom of God and the kingdom of Satan.

We must be of one mind to complete our singular mission—the growth and expansion of the kingdom of God and the simultaneous diminishing and destruction of the kingdom of darkness. Spiritual warfare is propelled by the Great Commission, the catalyst behind the expansion of the kingdom of God. This is why the various passages in the New Testament letters that make it clear that "we do not wrestle against flesh and blood" (Eph 6:12) have the principalities and powers in view, not demons.

The principalities and powers are the supernatural "princes" of Daniel 10. They are the "sons of God"—put over the nations at Babel in response to human disobedience to the Most High God (Deut 32:8)—who became wicked and corrupt, enslaving their populations, turning the hearts of humankind to idolatry (Ps 82). Though these sons of God were given their charges by the true God, their authority has been removed by that same God, the God of the Bible. The gospel calls everyone to forsake their gods and come back home. This is why New Testament writers link the resurrection of Jesus to the nullification of the authority of the rulers, authorities, and powers (Eph 1:15–23; 3:7–10; Col 2:13–15; 1 Pet 3:18–22).

From this perspective, spiritual warfare amounts to fulfilling one task: setting captive humanity free from the grip of this supernatural darkness through the gospel of Jesus Christ. Without the gospel, those under their power will die, estranged from God, owned by the original rebel, the lord of the dead.

Ephesians 6:10–18, one of the primary passages in the Bible describing spiritual warfare, supports these observations. Paul tells believers that "we do not wrestle against flesh and blood" (Eph 6:12). He exhorts his readers to "take up the whole armor of God" (Eph 6:13) to withstand the threat of the rulers, authorities, cosmic powers, and "spiritual forces of evil in the heavenly places" (Eph 6:12).

Nowhere (in this or other passages) does Paul recommend that believers confront or admonish the supernatural rulers and powers. His list of weapons does not include exorcism or rebuke of spiritual forces of evil. Instead, here is what Paul considered effective in spiritual combat against the forces of darkness elsewhere in the passage (Eph 6:13–18):

- truth (v. 14)

- righteousness (v. 14)

- the gospel (v. 15)

- faith (v. 16)

- salvation (v. 17)

- the word of God (v. 17)

- prayer and supplication (v. 18)

## THE RIGHT-SIDE UP

For Paul, spiritual warfare was about having persevering faith in the gospel and the word of God and living a holy, prayerful life as a follower of Jesus. It was about believers, those people who would never be the same again, collectively working to bring people still estranged from God back into the family, restoring what was lost when supernatural rebels deceived and corrupted his children. The kingdom of darkness must recede; the kingdom of God must increase.

As in *Stranger Things*, when we gain a clear focus of what must be done and work together as one mind, each performing the task set before us by the gifting and timing of God, we will overcome the darkness.

# 11

## I'LL BE
## WATCHING YOU

# THE ENDURING ENEMY

**A**fter several episodes of unresolved tension and constant threat, season 2 of *Stranger Things* ends with one of the happiest moments of the series: the Snow Ball at Hawkins Middle School. It's a memorable scene in so many ways. The comedic Dustin shows up at the middle school dance as miniature Steve, complete with curly mullet. But instead of working romantic magic, it repels the girls. Seemingly everyone else, even Will—now affectionately known as "Zombie Boy"—finds someone to dance with. Dustin shuffles to the side, alone and in tears. Nancy's sweet gesture, taking him out on the floor and giving him some confidence, is the best moment of the Snow Ball for me. Most fans, though, would likely single out as the cinematic pinnacle Eleven's fashionably late appearance and the look in Mike's eyes when he sees her. Their exchange and the brief kiss that follows are awkward and completely genuine.

## THE WATCHER

But the Snow Ball isn't truly the final scene. The Duffer brothers, the show's creators, didn't intend for solely images of adolescent romance to flutter nostalgically back into our minds while waiting for their next installment. Instead, our view of Hawkins Middle School slowly turns to reveal its Upside Down counterpart, climaxing with a glimpse of the Shadow Monster, exposed for a fleeting moment against the backdrop of a single flash of fire, bent menacingly over the school. The Watcher is the last thing we see.

The final minute of the Snow Ball scene actually sets the stage for this final image. The song for the slow dance is expertly chosen: "Every Breath You Take" by The Police. The lyrics that drift into our ears tell us what the Duffer brothers want us to know: the Watcher is watching. Something—*someone*—it wants has escaped its grasp and shut it out, and it wants her back. That the song begins at the moment Eleven enters the festively decorated gym is no coincidence. The visual capstone to season 2 tells us quite clearly that the Shadow Monster, the Mind Flayer, is not gone. It has suffered a defeat and indignantly watches its adversary from somewhere just behind the veil.

## IN THE COSMIC CROSSHAIRS

Unlike the ending of season 1, where Will coughed up a harbinger of things to come, alerting him to the fact that he was far from safe, there is no clear indication that any of the characters at the Snow Ball suspect the evil one still lingers. The Gate is closed. The doors of Hawkins lab were locked immediately thereafter. Hopper has custody of Eleven. If any of the characters wonder if they're truly safe, we get no such impression. All we know for sure is that they are certainly *not* out of harm's way, especially Eleven.

Aside from Eleven, two other characters could be perceived by the Watcher as lost prey: Will and Hopper. Are they also to be hunted by the Shadow? Are their fates connected?

It is suggestive that both of them are connected to Eleven in ways the other characters are not. Of the two, Hopper is the most transparent in this regard. Still grieving over the loss of little Sara years earlier, Hopper has filled the void with Eleven.

His heart is knit to her. From the time we watch Hopper reading to Eleven from *Anne of Green Gables*—the same book we see him reading to Sara before her untimely death—to the scene where they descend together into the abyss to close the Gate, we know their bond is real despite its difficulties.

In the season 2 finale, as they glimpse the enormous breach into the Upside Down, Eleven appears short of breath. Startled, she takes Hopper's hand as a low, ominous growl emanates from behind the glowing crack in the blackness. They don't separate until the moment is upon them, both visibly alarmed by the gargantuan form that takes shape behind the veil. Together they do what must be done. Eleven overcomes the Shadow while Hopper keeps its minions at bay. After the crisis passes, Hopper is covertly designated as Eleven's father (Dr. Owens hands him a birth certificate for Eleven, not a certificate of adoption). Their destinies are inextricably linked.

Eleven's connection to Will is more cryptic. Many fans have pointed out that the stuffed animal lion in Eleven's room at Hawkins lab is identical to one that we see in Castle Byers when Eleven, assisted by the makeshift sensory deprivation pool, finds Will. (Fan theories that posit that Sara's stuffed animal is also the same are incorrect; hers has stripes and is clearly a tiger.) In season 2 Eleven tells Joyce she knows Will is suffering because she's "seen" him. There appears to be a psychic (and perhaps historical) attachment between the two.

## SOMEONE ELSE WATCHING?

In addition to the potentially unknown fates of Hopper and Will, the specter of "Papa"—the twisted Dr. Brenner—still looms over Eleven. Season 2 begins with the premise that Brenner is dead, killed by the Demogorgon in the showdown at Hawkins Middle School. Eleven certainly believes this. It's one of the reasons, as the vision of Brenner implanted by Kali in Eleven's mind tells her, that she never attempts to see him through the Upside Down. Brenner perversely reveals another reason: maybe she was afraid of what she would find.

We can't know for sure if Kali made up the dialogue for her vision of Brenner. But the truth is that we never actually see Brenner die at the end of season 1. The Demogorgon leaps on him, but neither his death nor his body are ever shown, even in flashbacks. Dr. Owens, the one person who should know, comments on Brenner obliquely on two occasions. His language is (intentionally?) imprecise. He never says Brenner is dead, only "gone." When Jonathan tells Nancy that the people who were responsible for what happened to Will are all dead, she challenges him: "Do you really believe that?"

Ray Carroll certainly doesn't—or he's an exceptional liar. While his name may be unfamiliar, viewers would find him hard to forget. Ray was the man Kali prodded Eleven to kill in the seventh episode of season 2, one of the "bad men" who hurt the girls and, more pointedly, had been responsible for lobotomizing Eleven's mother. "You hurt Momma," Eleven accuses him angrily. Trying to justify his actions, Ray gasps, "I just did what he told me to do. He said she was sick." Kali will have none of it: "You had a choice, Ray, and you chose to follow a man you knew was evil." Ray begs for his life by telling the girls he can help them by leading them to Brenner. Eleven tells him, "Papa is gone," but Ray insists otherwise: "No, he's alive ... I'm not lying ... he trusts me. I'll take you to him."

In the wake of all this, there are good reasons to wonder if Brenner is also watching Eleven from a distance. If he is, he's more of a threat than one would suppose. In the scene where Kali fabricates the vision of Brenner, the mirage tells Eleven:

You have to confront your pain.

You have a wound, Eleven, a terrible wound.

And it's festering.

Do you remember what that means? Festering?

It means a rot.

And it will grow.

... And eventually, it will kill you.

As I acknowledge above, it may be the case that these words are better understood as those of Kali. After all, they come from her elsewhere in the episode. But just before the Demogorgon appeared in Hawkins Middle School at the end of season 1, Brenner whispered to Eleven, "You're sick, but I'm going to make you better. I'm going to take you back home, where I can make you well again. Where we can make all of this better." If Brenner is indeed alive, there's little doubt he will seek to manipulate Eleven emotionally and psychologically in an attempt to turn her away from Mike, the Party, Hopper, and everyone else.

Season 2 thus ends with Eleven vulnerable to threats from without and within. That should sound familiar. As we discussed earlier, Christians are confronted on the same two fronts.

## STAYING ON COURSE

Our spiritual enemies have not lost sight of us. The devil is our adversary, who "prowls around like a roaring lion, seeking someone to devour" (1 Pet 5:8). We are to surrender no ground to him (Eph 4:27), resisting his "schemes" (Eph 6:11). Peter goes on to tell us, "Resist him, firm in your faith, knowing that the same kinds of suffering are being experienced by your brotherhood throughout the world" (1 Pet 5:9). Paul reminds us, "We do not wrestle against flesh and blood, but against the rulers, against the authorities, against the cosmic powers over this present darkness, against the spiritual forces of evil in the heavenly places" (Eph 6:12).

Within, we struggle against our flesh, the forces resident within our unredeemed bodies that oppose our growth as believers and impede our effectiveness for the mission of the gospel. We lament with Paul:

> For I know that nothing good dwells in me, that is, in my flesh. For I have the desire to do what is right, but not the ability to carry it out. For I do not do the good I want, but the evil I do not want is what I keep on doing. Now if I do what I do not want, it is no longer I who do it, but sin that dwells within me. (Rom 7:18-20)

We have been grafted into Christ through his victory over death. We have received his Spirit to help us follow Jesus and work to fulfill the Great Commission (Matt 28:18-20; Rom 15:16-19; 1 Thess 1:5). Those are present foretastes of what is to come. We are partakers of the divine nature right now, rescued from the corruption of this age (2 Pet 1:4), members of Christ's kingdom (Col 1:13), set apart by the word of the gospel (John 17:17). Yet we are still in this world though not of the world (John 17:14-16). We live and partner with God in this present age, awaiting the blessed hope, the age to come (Titus 1:2; 2:13).

## THE RIGHT-SIDE UP

Like the characters of *Stranger Things* at the end of season 2, Christians cannot be lulled into forgetting that we face unseen threats. Watchfulness is key for continuing in our faith and for playing our role in God's grand objective to reclaim lost children for everlasting membership in his family. Within our own ranks and with respect to our own lives, we must:

- "be watchful, stand firm in the faith" (1 Cor 16:13)

- "keep watch on yourself, lest you too be tempted" (Gal 6:1)

- "continue steadfastly in prayer, being watchful in it with thanksgiving" (Col 4:2)

- "keep a close watch" on our doctrine (1 Tim 4:16)

- "watch out for those who cause divisions and create obstacles contrary to the doctrine that you have been taught" (Rom 16:17).

Ultimately, the Bible reminds us that we can trust God and his Spirit to help us resist the unseen threats set against us. A greater Power loves us, sent his Son for us, sees us (Job 34:21; Ps 33:13), and continues to care for us (1 Cor 8:3; 2 Tim 2:19).

# EPILOGUE

## BACK TO THE FUTURE:
## THE MESSAGE OF SEASON 3 ... AND 4

Like millions of other fans, my Fourth of July had been scripted months before the day arrived. Netflix® gave fans ample lead time by announcing that would be the day it released the latest installment of *Stranger Things*.

I wasn't disappointed. Although the story line developed more slowly than its predecessors, season 3 delivered the goods. Several expected changes for the characters and equally predictable plot trajectories from the earlier seasons made their appearance. Among those, one emerged transcendent, orienting the entire season and, I strongly suspect, the season to come. In so doing, it provided a metaphor for the present state of the believing church as it faces the threat—and hope—of the future.

### SOME THINGS CHANGE

As we saw earlier, in season 2 both Hopper and Jonathan Byers lamented that nothing would ever be the same. The contexts were Will's ordeal, the loss of Eleven, the fate of Barb, and the fear of the government spooks behind Hawkins lab. Joyce had her son back, but it became obvious that something was wrong. And one careless word of truth about what really had happened in Hawkins would have devastating consequences for the lives of everyone involved.

Season 3 opens in an ostensibly lighter mood. It is morning in Hawkins. Steve, Nancy, and Jonathan are out of high school and becoming responsible adults. Nancy and Jonathan are getting paid to start careers we know they like, photography and journalism. Sure, the men they work for are jerks, but they can put up with the belittling, at least for now. While Steve's job at Scoops Ahoy! is crummy—and wonderfully farcical—it beats battling Demogorgons. He is alive and a folk hero to a handful of awkward kids ... who aren't kids anymore. Mike and Eleven are together at last. So are Lucas and Max. Even Dustin has a girlfriend (Suzie), hundreds of miles away in Mormon country, though everyone else in the Party doubts she is real. And Hawkins has moved into the big time—it has a *mall*!

Despite the promises of young love and a closed gate, it isn't long before the mood changes. Kids grow up, and in the course of doing so, relationships shift and transform, steered by emerging adulthood. Will is again lost, but this time in *his* world. He doesn't have a girlfriend and doesn't want one. The new normal isn't cutting it. He misses the D&D marathons. He misses his friends. Sure, they are all there, but they aren't present in his life the way they had been.

The "here but not here" theme is most vividly propelled by Dustin. His first appearance in the new season comes on the way home from Camp Knowhere, a summer getaway for science geeks. After a month-long absence, his radio calls are not acknowledged ("This is Gold Leader returning to base"). While the radio silence didn't mean indifference (his friends were waiting to surprise him at his house), the growing distance between Party members surfaces quickly. His friends climb "Weathertop" hill to watch him assemble Cerebro, an oversized ham radio he made at camp, but their interest isn't sustained. Mike and Eleven pair off to go make out at her place. Max, Lucas, and Will give up on waiting for Dustin's girlfriend to respond. Will captures the moment as he leaves: "Maybe tomorrow we can play D&D, or something fun … like we used to." But when Dustin goes to see Steve at the mall the next day, he isn't reunited with the Party until episode 7. The Party seems to be disintegrating.

Will's pain was immediately familiar to me. Change is a necessary part of life, but it can really stink. I can recall vividly the night I fully realized that going to college meant leaving behind my best friend—someone I had known since I was nine, the boy who had introduced me to Jesus. It was, in a word, traumatic. And my return for the summer didn't cure anything. There was no time to do the things we had always done, like play football on weekends and the baseball board game (APBA) that absorbed us almost every waking moment as kids. I was home, but it wasn't home.

Like Will, Hopper and Joyce are struggling, too. For the first time in the show's history, Hopper is at a loss over what to do in a crisis. He made all the right calls in the search for Will. His continued distrust of Hawkins lab and his intuition about the subterranean rot under his town had been spot-on. But at the outset of season 3 he is confronted with a greater challenge: raising a teenage daughter (and one that has telekinetic powers to boot). His waistline shows the effect of too many evenings sitting outside Eleven's room pretending to watch TV while consuming Doritos and beer, searching for a way to keep Mike away from the house. Our reckless hero has a new identity: a distressed dad.

Joyce isn't grabbing any gusto, either. In the first episode of season 3 we glimpse the crayon drawing of Bob Newby that we saw at the end of season 2 after his tragic death. It's still on Joyce's refrigerator door. Fans of the show expected that she and Hopper would be together by now, but that just isn't happening. When Hopper shows up at Melvald's General Store for advice about his daughter and winds up inviting Joyce to dinner, she tells him she has plans and extricates herself from the conversation. Patsy Cline's "She's Got You" plays on the soundtrack. Hopper obviously loves her, but she's committed to her own rendezvous with the television, picking her way through warmed-up lasagna and canned peas. She can't get Bob out of her head. Change hurts.

## OTHER THINGS STAY THE SAME

It's no surprise that what doesn't change from the first two seasons is the evil that will ultimately confront the characters. Season 3 gives us both human and supernatural evil, once again inextricably entwined. The villains of Hawkins lab are gone, replaced by the quintessential 80s threat: the godless Russian Commies.

Season 2 ended with the immense, spidery silhouette of the Shadow Monster looming over the Upside Down's version of Hawkins Middle School. Eleven had arrived. He had found his prey. In season 3 we learn very quickly that closing the gate had not entirely eliminated the otherworldly reach of the Shadow Monster into the human realm. The Russians have secretly built an underground base beneath Starcourt Mall to reopen the gate. (They somehow know that a successful breech into the alternate reality had occurred in Hawkins—a point of knowledge that has troubling implications for what to expect in season 4.) Their efforts serve the Shadow's plan for revenge.

With darkness incarnate energized in season 3, the hive mind is once again awakened. But this time there are no Demodogs. The form taken by the hive mind this time around was presciently but unknowingly telegraphed by Dustin in the penultimate episode of season 2. Drawing on his knowledge of the *D&D Expert Rulebook*, the Party's Bard had introduced the "Mind Flayer" as an analogy of the enemy they were facing. In response to Hopper's question about what would kill the Mind Flayer, Dustin had replied, "You summon an undead army, uh, because ... because zombies, you know, they don't have brains, and the Mind Flayer, it ... it likes brains." In a dark inversion of Dustin's assessment, in season 3 it is the Mind Flayer who creates an undead army. It begins by harvesting the rodents of the town's outskirts but soon moves on to larger game.

The Mind Flayer's first human host is Billy Hargrove, Max's stepbrother. His debut in season 2 made him an obvious choice for villainy as the show moved on. Billy is out of control, driven by pain and rage, the roots of which are revealed in season 3. On his way to a lusty encounter with an older, married woman (Mrs. Wheeler, Nancy's mom), Billy crashes his car after an unseen missile of goo sent from the Mind Flayer shatters his windshield. Once out of the car, Billy is snatched by a tentacle and dragged into the bowels of the abandoned Brimborn Steelworks building. He becomes a tool for capturing other victims, bringing them to the creature's lair for assimilation. Hawkins is soon infested with zombies who think and act as an obedient, relentless collective. In a sickening plot twist, the hive's zombies can dissolve and combine into an amorphous blob that in turn assumes the physical presence of the Shadow, a freakish amalgam of semi-digested flesh and bone.

The Shadow's tactics are strategic and intentional. It knows that eventually its nemesis will seek answers, especially when Billy starts drawing attention. In episode 6, Eleven searches for the missing townspeople (the "Flayed") in the Void, the visual representation of her mind, her field of extrasensory perception. Her success in detecting Billy brings with it the realization that the Mind Flayer is laying a trap. A flashback to the memory of her encounter with Momma in the Void prompts Eleven to try to circumvent the snare by visiting Billy's past, not his present, in the hope that she can learn the Mind Flayer's whereabouts— the "Source," as the characters call it.

But the Shadow has learned from Eleven's earlier exploits. As soon as Eleven approaches Billy in the Void, the scene switches to "present Billy," aware that he is being viewed. When Eleven asks permission to see his memories, he grabs her arm threateningly, then releases her as she struggles, sending her falling into the past. Eleven gets the necessary information about the Source, and in so doing she is witness to the physical and emotional abuse inflicted on him by his father. But even more troubling is the realization that, by venturing into the Source, she has exposed herself to the Mind Flayer's own sight. When she tries to return to the present, the Mind Flayer temporarily delays her passage back to the present to deliver an eerie message through Billy:

> You shouldn't have looked for me, because now I see you. Now we can all see you. You let us in, and now you are going to have to let us stay. Don't you see? All this time, we've been building it. We've been building it … for you. All that work, all that pain … all of it … for you. And now it's time. Time to end it. And we are going to end *you*. And when you are gone, we are going to end your friends. And then we are going to end … *everyone*.

The agenda isn't new. In the very first episode of season 2, as Will struggles to explain his visions to Dr. Owens at Hawkins lab, the scientist asks, "What do you think the evil wanted?" Will replies: "To kill … not me; *everyone* else."

# PERIL AND PROVIDENCE

There are several insightful lessons about God's providential work in the lives of those he seeks to be in his family—*everyone*—in season 3. Recall that in the biblical story, both the members of the heavenly host and human beings were created by God to be *like* God and *with* God in their respective realms, heaven and earth. But these gifts weren't enough for some of God's children. They fell short of *being* God.

Tragically, the biblical story of those created to bear the image of God is one driven by the urge for autonomy, the impulse to reject heavenly authority. The Bible's overarching story, its metanarrative, speaks of failure in Eden, expulsion from God's home, transgression of the boundary between heaven and earth, God's abandonment of humanity at Babel, the corruption of the sons of God allotted as caretakers of the nations, and a world engulfed by chaos of both human and supernatural causation. When God's children in heaven or earth want more than he wills, the result is death, depravity, and destruction, personally and corporately.

The first two seasons of *Stranger Things* illustrated that chaos in memorable ways. Season 3 follows suit.

For example, the Russian quest to open the Gate serves as a metaphor for the human ambition to recover what was willfully rejected so long ago, to have Eden on one's own terms, to tap the divine realm for its secrets, to be gods. Such efforts always fail, while providence reigns.

In this instance, the code used by the Russians to get the fuel that runs the supermachine (a "key") used to open the Gate is broken by three teenagers after being accidentally intercepted by Dustin's ham radio. The same device later allows Dustin to guide Hopper, Joyce, and Murray inside the base. Cerebro operates on a frequency that no one in the Russian military expects since the American military doesn't use shortwave. The device is also crucial for obtaining the numerical sequence of Planck's Constant, produced by Dustin's very real girlfriend Suzie, the Mormon math whiz he met at Camp Knowhere, after he signals her in one last desperate plea in the season finale.

*Stranger Things* of course presents all of this as serendipitous, the product of chance. But the unlikely series of circumstances is actually a wonderful illustration of providence. Once again, human evil is unable to anticipate how its aims could be undermined, compromised, and overturned. The reason is simple: humans can never see the full picture. Only God sees all the players, knows all their abilities and propensities, and understands all the potential interactions and outcomes. And God is no disinterested, passive onlooker. He *seeks* the good for those who love him and the redemption of those who do not.

The supernatural hive mind suffers the same liability. Its very nature is its own weakness. The hive mind operates *within* the collective. It is a closed system. It is like a self-programming computer that omits and overlooks all instructions that do not derive from and perpetuate the collective. It has no way to anticipate outlier thoughts; it can only react to them after the fact and learn. A hive mind cannot out-maneuver the non-hive mind. Intelligent evil is no match for the unseen hand of providence.

In the climax of season 3, the Mind Flayer never anticipates the efforts underway to close the Gate again. Ironically, its fate was sealed the night it took Billy.

The monster used Billy as bait to entrap Eleven. She knowingly takes the risk and suffers the consequences. But the Mind Flayer never suspects that her decision to contact Billy in the Void might create the path to its own downfall. It can only think of revenge. It never foresees, as Billy lays the stricken girl before its fiendish maw, that Eleven's compassion could penetrate Billy's enslaved mind long enough to release the memory of his forgotten happiness, turning his heart to save her and surrender his own life to buy Joyce and Hopper enough time to close the Gate. It fails and dies precisely because it was a hive mind. Its vision was too limited, and so, consumed by its own hubris and hatred for Eleven, it was blind to its own impending demise.

## PRESENT AND FUTURE HOPE
## ... AND THREAT

While Eleven's life was saved and the Gate once again sealed, season 3 nevertheless ended with two shockers: the apparent death of Hopper, and Eleven losing her powers. I strongly suspect the two are tied together and will be in the next season. My intention here isn't to contribute more fan theories to an already mushrooming mass of chatter. Instead, I would like to focus on one of these developments and offer some food for thought to those who embrace the gospel.

I'm no different than any other fan of *Stranger Things*. The ending of the third season set my mind reeling. Given that Eleven is clearly a Christ figure in the show, the loss of her powers makes no sense. Granted, I don't think the spiritual analogies I've discussed in this book were intended by its creators—and that's what honestly makes them more intriguing. It's as if a greater Writer wants to communicate truths through the skilled artistry of the show. It should be obvious by now that I believe that much is on the table. Consequently, I think the same holds true for this unexpected twist. The issue isn't what the Duffer brothers are thinking—it's how God might use their art.

The conclusion I've come to is that the loss of Eleven's powers is not commentary on her. The loss conveys no theological messaging about Jesus or the gospel itself. Rather, I see a metaphor about the believing church at large—which is him, in a sense.

Put simply, in biblical thought, the believing church is Christ's body (Eph 5:23; Col 1:18, 24). The body of Christ is indwelt by the Spirit of God (1 Cor 6:19–20), who empowers it to carry out the Great Commission, the command of the risen Christ to spread the gospel, making disciples of all nations (Matt 28:18–20; Rom 12:4–8; Eph 3:14–18). The body of Christ is portrayed in the book of Acts as an irresistible force, succeeding against all odds and despite persecution. Believers were united in supporting each other, single-minded in mission. They blessed their enemies and were willing to suffer—a testimony of love so powerful that, eventually, their persecutors joined their ranks. In biblical theology, the body of Christ on earth is to be Jesus to the world, to be the antidote to chaos, to be a glimpse of life the way God originally wanted it for his children—to be a loving, accepting home, bearing each other's burdens and sharing the presence of God.

Let me be blunt: Is this the church you see and experience?

Perhaps the more telling question is another one: Is this the church you expect to see as we head into the future?

Most Christians today, especially in the West, would be compelled by honesty to say no in both respects. It was hard to think of a powerless Eleven, the Christ representation of *Stranger Things,* and not be reminded that the body of Christ has lost its power. For me, the image of Eleven unable to get a box off the top shelf of the closet while packing up is the lingering point of reference in my mind.

The claim to have an exclusive means of salvation, though transparently biblical (John 14:6), has been the target of contempt for a very long time in modern thought. But the West is now actually transitioning to something more threatening: a *post-Christian* culture. As a fan of *Stranger Things*, if you've wondered how in the world the heroes of the show are going to face the next threat from the Upside Down *without* Eleven's powers, you now have the metaphor for considering the future of the church in an increasingly intolerant world.

But if we've learned any spiritual lesson from the analogies provided in the show, it's that providence reigns. And it will again. But that doesn't mean it won't be hard, and even scary. The church seems to be headed into the same sort of antagonistic world as the first followers of Jesus experienced. The small band of disciples left on earth to spread the gospel was surrounded by enemies, many of them lethal. The church of today is headed into the past—or should I say, *back to the future*?

No one who grew up in the 80s who had seen *Back to the Future* could miss the fact that the movie played a prominent role in season 3. Take the scene where Steve, Robin, Dustin, and Erica hide in the mall theater after escaping from the Russian base. What's playing? *Back to the Future.* Listening to Steve and Robin talk about the movie's time-travel plot is arguably one of the funniest scenes in the show's history. (You get the impression Steve would be totally flummoxed even without the drugs.) Other details overlap, too; for example, Mrs. Driscoll owns a black Kit-Cat clock just like Doc Brown in *Back to the Future* (and we had one in my house, too).[1]

I think it's obvious that the creators of *Stranger Things* expect fans of the show to discern that *Back to the Future* will be an orienting point for season 4. As such, there's a real message for

---

1. For other *Back to the Future* Easter eggs in season 3, see "Stranger Things 3: All the Hidden (and not-so-hidden) Film and TV References," The Telegraph, July 9, 2019, https://www.telegraph.co.uk/tv/0/stranger-things-3-hidden-not-so-hidden-film-tv-references2/back-future/.

those of us who follow Christ. The church is indeed going back to the future. Frankly, *it must.* The only way for the body of Christ to not merely survive but to thrive in the coming dark times of a post-Christian world is to return to its roots. The church must return to a time when it didn't have the luxury of infighting over peripheral points of interpretation, when the metanarrative of Scripture took center stage, when the body of Christ was not fragmented, and when every believer eagerly played their role in the one defining mission given to the body by its head, Jesus.

I suspect that Eleven will regain her powers and that the cost may be high. But I also suspect that her story will end the way the Bible has scripted the destiny of the body of Christ: what's lost will be restored, and life will not only return to the way it was but will be even better than she can imagine.

# SUBJECT INDEX

# SCRIPTURE INDEX

## OLD TESTAMENT

# NEW TESTAMENT